CONTEMPORARY

INTERMEDIATE 2

reading
basics

A REAL-WORLD APPROACH TO LITERACY

D1611466

Mc Graw Hill Education

Bothell, WA • Chicago, IL • Columbus, OH • New York, NY

Image Credits: Cover Lisa Fukshansky/The McGraw-Hill Companies

---

www.mheonline.com

 **Education**

Send all inquiries to:
Contemporary/McGraw-Hill
130 East Randolph Street, Suite 400
Chicago, IL 60601

ISBN: 978-0-07-659098-8
MHID: 0-07-659098-4

Printed in the United States of America.

1 2 3 4 5 6 7 8 9 QDB 15 14 13 12 11

Contents

UNIT 1

Lesson 1.1

Lesson 1.2

Lesson 1.3

Lesson 1.4

Lesson 1.5

Lesson 1.6

Lesson 1.7

UNIT 2

Lesson 2.1

Lesson 2.2

To the Student

Reading Basics will help you become a better reader. Research in evidence-based reading instruction (EBRI) has shown that reading has four important components, or parts: comprehension, alphabetics, vocabulary, and fluency. *Reading Basics* provides evidence-based reading instruction and practice in all four components. With your teacher's help, you can use the *Student Edition* and the articles in the *Intermediate 2 Reader* to gain important skills.

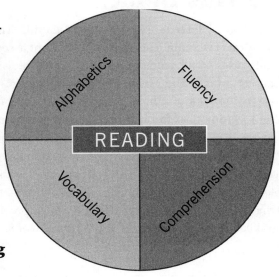

The Four Components of Reading

Comprehension *Reading Basics* teaches you many ways to improve your reading comprehension. Each lesson in the *Student Edition* introduces a different reading comprehension skill. You apply the skill to passages and to a workplace document. You also apply the skill to the articles in the *Reader*. Your teacher will help you use monitoring and fix-up reading strategies. You will learn ways to clarify your understanding of passages that are confusing to you. In addition, each article in the *Reader* begins with a before-reading strategy. At the end of the article, you will complete comprehension and critical thinking exercises.

Alphabetics In the *Student Edition* lessons, you will learn and practice alphabetics. Alphabetics includes phonics and word analysis skills, such as recognizing *r*-controlled vowels and syllable patterns, correctly spelling possessives and word endings, and studying word parts, such as prefixes, suffixes, base words, and roots. You can use alphabetics skills to help you read and understand difficult words. For more practice, go to www.mhreadingbasics.com and use *PassKey*. This online program provides skills instruction and guided feedback..

Vocabulary Studying academic vocabulary will help you as a learner. Your teacher will present and explain five academic vocabulary words that you will need to understand as you read each *Student Edition* lesson. You will have a chance to practice these words along with other important vocabulary skills such as recognizing and using synonyms, antonyms, and context clues.

   Your teacher will also present and explain vocabulary words important to your understanding of the articles in the *Reader*. As you read each article, notice that some words are defined in the margins. Use the definition and the context of each word to help you understand it.

Fluency Your teacher will present activities to help you with fluency—that is, reading smoothly, quickly, and accurately. You will practice fluency with the passages in the *Student Edition* and the articles in the *Reader*. You can also go to www.mhreadingbasics. com to download MP3 recordings of the articles. Listening to fluent reading will help you develop your own fluency skills.

How to Use This Book

The *Student Edition* consists of 19 lessons split among three units. These lessons help prepare you for questions on classroom tests and on important assessments. Each lesson is eight pages long and focuses on a particular reading comprehension skill.

Begin by taking the Pretest. Use the Answer Key to check your answers. Circle any wrong answers and use the Evaluation Chart to see which skills you need to practice.

Your teacher will guide your class through each lesson in the book. You will have chances to practice and apply skills on your own and in small groups. At the end of each unit, complete the Unit Review and Assessment. The Assessment will help you check your progress. Your teacher may want to discuss your answers with you.

After you complete the lessons in the book, you will take the Posttest on pages 189–198. The Evaluation Chart and Answer Key on pages 199–200 will help you see how well you have mastered the skills. To achieve mastery, you must answer 80 percent of the questions correctly.

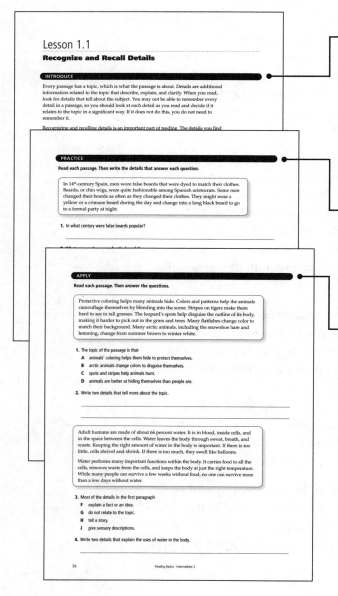

Working through Each Lesson

Introduce The first page of each lesson presents the reading skill. It also includes an example. Your teacher will use this example to explain and model the skill. Then your teacher will work with your class to do the guided practice at the bottom of the page. You will have a chance to practice this skill in the activities. Later in the lesson you will apply this skill to a document similar to one that you might use in the workplace.

Practice Next comes a page for practice. Usually, you will read a passage and answer questions about it that relate to the reading skill. You may be asked to fill out a graphic organizer to respond to a question. On some pages, there will be several passages followed by questions.

Apply The Apply page gives you a chance to apply the reading skill in a different way. In many lessons, you will read a passage and answer questions about it. You will see a variety of formats, including open-ended questions and graphic organizers.

Check Up The last page in the reading skills section of the lesson is the Check Up page. The questions on this page are always presented in a multiple-choice format. The Check Up page allows your teacher to monitor your progress as you learn the reading skill. Then your teacher can help you if you still have questions about the skill.

Workplace Skill The Workplace Skill page gives you another chance to practice the reading skill. Instead of using a reading passage, this page introduces the types of documents that you might find or need to use in the workplace. There could be a memo, a section of a handbook, or some kind of graph. You will read or study the document and answer questions about it.

The Workplace Skill documents relate to a wide variety of jobs. Some may be familiar to you, while others may be new.

Write for Work A Write for Work activity is at the top of the next page. You will do workplace-related writing such as drafting a memo or a set of procedures. The writing relates to the document on the Workplace Skill page. This activity provides a chance for you to practice your writing skills and reading comprehension at the same time.

Reading Extension In most lessons, a Reading Extension comes next. Here you apply the reading skill to an article in the *Reader*. After reading the article, you will answer multiple-choice and open-ended questions.

Workplace Extension Some lessons have a Workplace Extension instead of a Reading Extension. The Workplace Extension addresses work-related issues. These might include interviewing for a job or dealing with criticism at work. You will read a scenario in which a person is faced with a work problem or issue. Then you will answer questions about how the person handled the situation or what he or she should do next.

For each unit, your teacher will hand out a Workplace Skill Activity sheet. You will work with a partner or in small groups to practice skills similar to those in the Workplace Extension. Many of these activities include role-playing so that you can practice realistic conversations about the workplace.

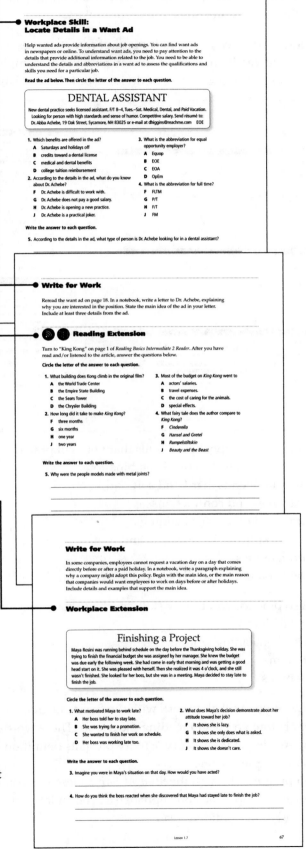

Explore Words You will practice two important reading skills in the Explore Words section of the lesson—alphabetics and vocabulary.

Each Explore Words section includes four or five activities. Each activity begins with brief instruction followed by practice. You may be asked to complete matching exercises, circle word parts, fill in missing words, or divide words into syllables.

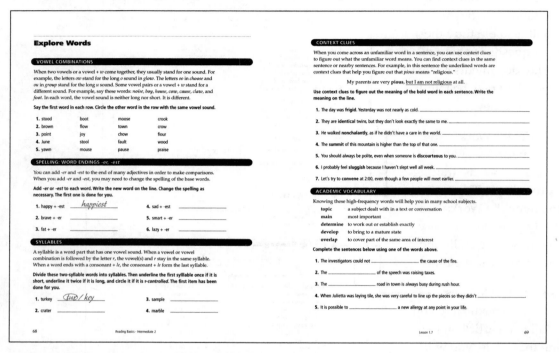

Here are some of the alphabetics skills that you will practice:
- *r*-controlled vowels, vowel combinations
- consonant blends, hard and soft *c* and *g*
- possessives and contractions
- plurals and other word endings
- prefixes, suffixes, base words, and roots
- word familiies
- syllable patterns and division

You will also practice vocabulary skills, such as these:
- context clues
- multiple-meaning words
- antonyms
- synonyms

In every lesson you will also work with the five academic vocabulary words your teacher will present before you begin reading the lesson. These words appear in context in the lesson. The Academic Vocabulary activity presents definitions of the words. You will use the words to complete sentences.

   As you progress through the *Student Edition* lessons, you will notice improvements in your reading comprehension, alphabetics, vocabulary, and fluency skills. You will be a stronger and more confident reader.

Pretest

Read each passage. Then circle the letter of the answer to each question.

> Sneezes spread germs, but some people have found that there's another hazard of sneezing. Drivers have reported having accidents or losing control of their cars because of sneezing. People who sneeze a lot because of allergies or colds can be putting themselves and others in danger. A sneeze takes all of a person's attention for several seconds. It's hard for anyone to keep his or her eyes open while sneezing. Often, drivers take their hands off the wheel to cover their noses and mouths when they sneeze. Therefore, a driver who sneezes multiple times loses sight of the road and possibly loses control of the car.

1. What is the main idea of this paragraph?

A A sneeze takes up a person's attention for several seconds.

B Sneezing is always hazardous.

C It is a good idea to stay out of cars if you have a cold.

D Sneezing while driving might be dangerous.

2. What is one possible effect of sneezing while driving?

F Drivers can develop allergies.

G Drivers can lose control of the car.

H Drivers can catch a cold.

J Drivers can focus better.

> Many gourmet cooks prefer white pepper to black pepper because white pepper has a milder flavor. Pepper plants bear small green berries that are picked as they start to turn a ripe red. To make black pepper, the berries, or peppercorns, are washed and dried in the sun. The berries' skins turn dark brown or black as they dry. Then the pepper is ground and packaged for sale. White pepper comes from the same berries. However, the outer coverings of the picked berries are softened for a few days and then removed by washing and rubbing or trampling the berries. The skinned berries are then spread in the sun to dry.

3. What causes white pepper to have a milder flavor than black pepper?

A White pepper berries are picked sooner than black pepper berries.

B White pepper berries are washed, and black peppercorns are not.

C The skin of white pepper berries has been removed.

D The white pepper berries are dried in the sun.

4. What is the best paraphrase of the first two sentences?

F Many cooks prefer white pepper because it is mild. It comes from the pepper plant.

G Pepper plants have small berries that turn red. They are picked. Then they become either white or black pepper.

H White pepper is milder than black pepper.

J Many cooks prefer white pepper because it is milder. Pepper berries are picked when they start to turn red.

Can certain colors make a person more creative or more attractive? According to some studies, the answer is yes. In one study, researchers gave 600 people tasks to do on computers. Some groups performed their tasks on computers with red backgrounds, while others used computers with blue backgrounds. The "red" groups performed better on tasks that tested memory, spelling, and punctuation. The "blue" groups performed better on tasks that required imagination, such as inventing toys from shapes. Another study wanted to know whether color makes people more attractive to others. Researchers showed photos of women to a group of men. The men thought the women who wore red shirts were more attractive than the women who wore other colors.

5. Which concept is stated in the passage?

   A   People who worked on blue computer screens performed better on tests that required imagination.

   B   People who worked on blue computer screens performed poorly on tests.

   C   More attractive people wear red clothing.

   D   People who live in red houses are more attractive.

6. Which is the best summary of this paragraph?

   F   Some research studies found that color can have an effect on creativity and attractiveness.

   G   Some research studies tested how color affects people. One study found that red screens improved performance on tasks involving memory, while blue screens improved performance on tasks involving imagination. Another study found that red clothing made women more attractive to men.

   H   Some research studies tested the effect of color on creativity. One study found that blue computer screens helped people perform better on tasks involving imagination.

   J   According to one study, women in red shirts were more attractive to men than women wearing other colors.

7. In what way were the two studies described in this passage alike?

   A   In both studies, participants preferred items that were red.

   B   Both studies looked at how color affects people.

   C   Both studies measured how well people did on tests.

   D   Both studies tested reactions to red and blue.

8. What was the writer's purpose for writing this passage?

   F   to explain why red is better than blue

   G   to describe two studies involving color

   H   to convince readers to use red backgrounds

   J   to convince women to wear red

According to Greek myth, Narcissus was a beautiful child who grew into a beautiful young man. One day, Narcissus was walking in the woods when he came to a pond with water so clear that it could have been glass. The water was free of grasses and weeds, and no creature disturbed the placid surface. When Narcissus bent down to take a drink from the beautiful pond, he saw his own reflection. He was instantly awestruck by the beautiful creature staring at him, and he couldn't help staring back. Narcissus was so happy just staring at his own lovely image that he forgot his need for food and drink. Narcissus stayed at the pond so long that he eventually died there. The Narcissus flower grew where he died.

9. Which character traits best describe Narcissus?

   A lazy and immature

   B hardworking and patient

   C foolish and vain

   D cold and selfish

10. From this passage you can conclude that the author's purpose is to

   F narrate a story about a happy young man.

   G caution readers about the dangers of vanity.

   H inspire others to appreciate their own looks.

   J describe why it is important to eat and drink.

The first paper money in North America was playing cards. At one time, people who lived in New France could buy tarts with the Queen of Hearts, and they could buy anything else with cards, too. In 1685 the French colonial government was running low on coins, so it started using cards from a standard playing deck as currency. The cards were signed by a government official and sent throughout French Quebec. This system was only supposed to be used until the real money arrived from France, but it stayed around for many more years because it was so popular.

11. Which is the main idea of this passage?

   A People who lived in New France could buy tarts with the Queen of Hearts.

   B The first paper money in North America was playing cards.

   C The French colonial government ran low on money.

   D The card money was signed by the governor.

12. Which sentence could be added to the paragraph to support the main idea?

   F By law, merchants had to accept cards as legal tender.

   G Five years later, the French and the English were at war.

   H Fur trade was the main economic activity in New France.

   J The French were great explorers.

Pretest continued

Read the glossary/index. Then circle the letter of the answer to each question.

Glossary/Index

gene   part of a chromosome that controls inherited traits, *14–54*

genetics   the study of heredity, *14–20*

gestation   the carrying of young inside its mother's body, *132–144*

gland   a part of the body that produces and secretes substances used by the body, *132*

habitat   the place where an organism lives, *115*

herbivore   an animal that eats only plants, *120–122*

heredity   passing of traits from parents to offspring, *14–54, 118–130*

13. What is most likely the genre of the book that contains this glossary?

   A fiction

   B drama

   C poetry

   D nonfiction

14. Where would you find information about habitats?

   F page 19

   G page 115

   H page 121

   J page 132

15. Suppose the writer wants to add the word *germinate* to the glossary. Which word would it come before?

   A genetics

   B gland

   C gestation

   D habitat

16. As used in the glossary, *young* means

   F "offspring."

   G "a creature that eats only meat."

   H "food."

   J "not old."

Read each passage. Then circle the letter of the answer to each question.

> Many people believe that if a fine tea is kept for too long, it becomes stale or spoiled. Some Chinese tea drinkers disagree, however. They say that good black teas are like fine wines. They claim that, like some wines, some black teas improve in flavor when they are aged. They say that the leaves transform from green to gold and finally to a dark brownish black over time. As the tea ages, layers of fruity and woody flavors appear that are not noticeable when the tea is young.

17. In this passage, good black tea is compared to

   A wine.

   B gold.

   C apples.

   D oak.

18. From this passage, you can conclude that

   F black tea is better than green tea.

   G there are different types of black tea.

   H some tea gets better as it gets older.

   J all black teas age well.

In spite of its name, a jellyfish is not a fish at all. While true fish have skeletons, jellyfish do not. A jellyfish's body is made up of 99% water, but what the jellyfish lacks in bones and other organs, it makes up for in stomach. Hanging from its body are stinging tentacles, which the jellyfish uses to capture prey. The box jellyfish is considered to be the deadliest jellyfish in the world. Its venom instantly stuns or kills prey such as fish and shrimp. Its sting is the most painful thing imaginable. Its sting is so painful that human victims have been known to go into shock and drown or die of heart failure before even reaching shore.

19. Which style technique does the writer use in the passage?

  A description

  B interruptions

  C dialogue

  D action

20. What do you predict will happen to prey after the jellyfish stings it?

  F The prey will turn into a skeleton.

  G The prey will turn into a jellyfish.

  H The prey will swim away.

  J The jellyfish will eat it.

21. Which sentence is an opinion?

  A A jellyfish's body is made up of 99% water.

  B While true fish have skeletons, jellyfish do not.

  C Its venom instantly stuns or kills prey such as fish and shrimp.

  D Its sting is the most painful thing imaginable.

22. What do jellyfish use to sting their victims?

  F tentacles

  G stomach

  H skeleton

  J organs

Early people often created myths and gods to explain natural events. Lightning and thunder, for example, must have been very frightening experiences. Many early religions had their own gods of thunder and lightning. Jupiter was the king of Roman gods and the god of thunder, lightning, and rain. Zeus was the Greek god of lightning. Thor, a Norse god, was also a god of weather. Whenever these gods were displeased with people or with other gods, they would throw thunderbolts, which were often accompanied by huge gusts of wind.

23. Based on the passage, what generalization can you make about how early people viewed their gods?

  A They thought their gods were frightening.

  B They thought their gods were powerless.

  C They thought their gods were responsible for weather events..

  D They thought their gods were caring.

24. What reference source could you use to find out more about Norse, Roman, and Greek gods?

  F an encyclopedia

  G an almanac

  H a dictionary

  J a thesaurus

Read the nutrition label. Then circle the letter of the answer to each question.

Nutrition Facts

Serving Size	1 medium potato (148g)
Servings Per Container	About 12

Amount Per Serving

Calories 110	Calories from Fat 0

	% Daily Value*
Total Fat 0g	0%
Saturated Fat 0g	0%
Cholesterol 0mg	0%
Sodium 0mg	0%
Potassium 620mg	18%
Total Carbohydrate 26g	9%
Dietary Fiber 2g	8%
Sugars 1g	
Protein 2g	

Vitamin A	0%	Vitamin C	45%
Calcium	2%	Iron	6%

*Percent Daily Values are based on a 2,000-calorie diet. Your daily values may be higher or lower depending on your calorie needs.

25. What can you conclude from the nutrition information on this label?

   A Potatoes are high in sugar.

   B Potatoes are a nonfat food.

   C Potatoes are high in salt.

   D Potatoes are a good source of vitamin A.

26. You would find this type of label on

   F a piece of furniture.

   G a food item.

   H a menu.

   J an appliance.

27. What is the recommended serving size?

   A 12 potatoes

   B one potato

   C one half of a potato

   D not stated

28. What reference source could you use to look up information about last year's potato crops?

   F dictionary

   G encyclopedia

   H world almanac

   J *Guinness World Records*

29. Which item would change for a person who eats 1,500 calories a day?

   A the servings per container

   B the calories in one serving

   C the size of one serving

   D the percentage of daily values

30. Of the nutrients listed, the one found in the highest percentage is

   F sodium

   G potassium

   H vitamin C

   J calcium

Pretest continued

Read the workplace document from a bus company's procedures manual. Then circle the letter of the answer to each question.

Rules for Drivers

1. No school bus driver will allow a passenger or other unauthorized person to operate the school bus at any time.

2. No person except the driver will be allowed to sit in the driver's seat.

3. No driver will leave the driver's seat without first setting the brakes, shutting off the motor, placing the bus in gear, and removing the ignition key. The driver will keep keys in his or her possession.

4. The driver will take care that passengers boarding or leaving the bus are within his or her view at all times. Therefore, the driver will **never** allow passengers to walk behind the bus.

5. No school bus driver will walk away from his or her bus while passengers are aboard.

6. Drivers will make sure that the windshield and rear window of the bus are clean.

7. Drivers will make sure that all brakes, lights, stop signs, warning signal lamps, and other safety devices are working properly before starting on any trip.

8. The speed of a school bus will never exceed the legal truck speed or any other posted speed limit.

---

31. The first thing a driver should do when leaving the bus is

   A shut off the motor.

   B remove the ignition key.

   C set the brakes.

   D place the bus in gear.

32. The writer's style creates an effect of

   F suspense.

   G humor.

   H uncertainty.

   J authority.

33. What is the fastest the bus driver is allowed to drive if the posted speed limit is 40 miles per hour?

   A 25 miles per hour

   B 30 miles per hour

   C 40 miles per hour

   D 50 miles per hour

34. Based on the document, which statement is a valid generalization?

   F School bus drivers must ensure passengers' safety.

   G Only the driver can sit in the driver's seat.

   H Drivers must get CPR training.

   J Drivers' uniforms must be in good condition.

35. What is the writer's purpose for writing this document?

   A to make sure bus drivers do not exceed the speed limit

   B to convince readers to become bus drivers

   C to explain the rules that bus drivers must follow

   D to entertain with a story about driving a bus

36. What could happen if a passenger walked behind the bus?

   F The driver could not see the passenger.

   G The passenger could trip and fall.

   H The driver could allow someone else to sit in the driver's seat.

   J The driver could not make sure the windows are clean.

Read the want ad from a local newspaper. Then circle the letter of the answer to each question.

Child Care Worker

Little Bears is a child care center that has served families in Madison for 23 years. We are looking for a child care worker to join our team.

This is a permanent, full-time position taking care of children who are six months to three years old. A key part of the role is planning and implementing high-quality, creative educational activities for children.

Applicants must be at least 18 years old and must agree to undergo a background check. To succeed in this position you will also need the following:

- at least one year experience working in child care
- first-aid and CPR certificates
- a genuine interest in working with children
- the ability to form warm, responsive relationships with children
- a positive, friendly attitude
- verbal and written communication skills
- initiative and ability to work with minimal supervision

Little Bears offers a competitive salary, and you will be working in great conditions.

To apply, please e-mail your résumé and cover letter to the managing director.

---

37. Which statement from the ad is an opinion?

   A Little Bears has served families for 23 years.

   B We are looking for a child care worker to join our team.

   C Applicants must be at least 18 years old.

   D You will be working in great conditions.

38. As used in the ad, *key* means

   F "a device that opens a lock."

   G "a button on a computer keyboard."

   H "of critical importance."

   J "the explanation for map symbols."

39. You apply for a job at this center. You like children but have never worked with them. What do you predict will happen?

   A You will be asked to take a first-aid course.

   B You will not be considered for the job.

   C You will be called to come in for an interview.

   D You will be asked to supply letters of recommendation.

40. How old are the children served by this child-care center?

   F three to five years old

   G three to six months old

   H three to six years old

   J six months to three years old

Pretest continued

Circle the letter of the word that is spelled correctly.

41. He skinned the _____ on his hand.

    A nuckels

    B knuckles

    C knuckels

    D nuckles

42. The parents of the sick child had many _____.

    F worries

    G worrys

    H wories

    J worryies

43. Del ate the _____ pizza by himself.

    A whol

    B hol

    C whole

    D whoal

44. _____ never ridden in a helicopter.

    F Ive

    G I'hve

    H I'hav

    J I've

45. If it rains, please close the _____.

    A windows

    B windowss

    C windowes

    D windowws

46. How many _____ of cookies did you bake?

    F batchs

    G batches

    H batchess

    J batchss

47. I broke my _____ when I fell off my bike.

    A wist

    B wrist

    C rist

    D wrrist

Circle the letter of the answer to each question.

48. Which two words are homophones?

    F were, wheel

    G wear, ware

    H wraps, warps

    J wings, whites

49. Which word means "to link together"?

    A superlink

    B linkist

    C linker

    D interlink

50. Which phrase means "the house belonging to the Walkers"?

    F the Walker's house

    G the Walkers house

    H the Walkers' house

    J the Walkers's house

51. Which word fits into both sentences?

    The manual gives all the _____ for putting the bike together.

    The ice has made the _____ slippery.

    A stairs

    B signs

    C instructions

    D steps

52. Which word does NOT have a long *o* vowel sound?

    F throw

    G growl

    H toast

    J broke

53. Which word begins with a consonant blend?

    A simple

    B carton

    C lantern

    D slippery

54. Which word means "of many cultures"?

   F multicultural

   G miscultural

   H semicultural

   J precultural

55. What is the meaning of the prefix *sub-*?

   A not

   B below

   C before

   D badly

56. Which word does NOT have an *r*-controlled vowel sound?

   F giraffe

   G sternest

   H crunchy

   J encore

57. Which word is a synonym for *disappointment*?

   A regret

   B appointment

   C delight

   D feeling

58. Which is an antonym of the word *interesting*?

   F charming

   G delightful

   H boring

   J knowledgeable

59. Which word means "someone who types"?

   A typist

   B typer

   C typor

   D typeser

60. Which two words are synonyms?

   F murky, unclear

   G silly, practical

   H shouted, whispered

   J ramble, climb

61. Which is the base word in the word *reappearance*?

   A reappear

   B reappeared

   C appear

   D appearance

62. Which word is the name of a vehicle with one wheel?

   F bicycle

   G tricycle

   H unicycle

   J semicycle

63. Which word begins with the same sound as *gypsy*?

   A garage

   B galloping

   C juicy

   D glutten

64. Which two words belong to the same word family?

   F visor, invisible

   G auditorium, cafeteria

   H relief, relax

   J blueberry, peach

Circle the letter of the word that completes each analogy.

65. *Shoe* : *foot* as *belt* : _____.

   F arm

   G neck

   H waist

   J wrist

66. *Shovel* : *digging* as _____ : *writing*.

   A book

   B pencil

   C paper

   D envelope

PRETEST EVALUATION CHART AND ANSWER KEY

This pretest was designed to help you determine which reading skills you need to study. This chart shows which skill is being covered with each test question. Use the key on page 12 to check your answers. Then circle the questions you answered incorrectly and go to the practice pages in this book covering those skills.

Tested Skills	Question Numbers	Practice Pages
Recognize and Recall Details	14, 22, 27, 30, 33, 40	14–17
Understand Stated Concepts	5	22–25
Draw Conclusions	18, 25	30–33
Summarize and Paraphrase	4, 6	38–41
Identify Cause and Effect	2, 3, 36	46–49
Identify Style Techniques	19	54–57
Find the Main Idea	1, 11	62–65
Identify Sequence	31	78–81
Understand Consumer Materials	25–30	86–89
Use Reference Sources/Indexes	13–16, 24, 28	94–97
Recognize Character Traits	9	102–105
Use Supporting Evidence	12	110–113
Identify Author's Purpose	8, 10, 35	118–121
Make Generalizations	23, 34	134–137
Identify Author's Effect and Intention	32	142–145
Compare and Contrast	7, 17	150–153
Predict Outcomes	20, 39	158–161
Identify Fact and Opinion	21, 37	166–169
Identify Genre	13	174–177
Synonyms/Antonyms	57, 58, 60	20, 28, 84, 124, 172
Context Clues	16, 38, 51	29, 45, 69, 93, 109, 141, 165
Spelling	41–48, 50	28, 37, 52, 60, 68, 85, 92, 100, 116, 124, 149, 180
Phonics/Word Analysis	49, 52–56, 59, 61–66	20, 21, 28, 36, 44, 52, 53, 60, 61, 68, 84, 92, 101, 108, 117, 124, 125, 140, 148, 156, 157, 164, 172, 173, 180, 181

	KEY		
1.	D	34.	F
2.	G	35.	C
3.	C	36.	F
4.	J	37.	D
5.	A	38.	H
6.	F	39.	B
7.	B	40.	J
8.	G	41.	B
9.	C	42.	F
10.	G	43.	C
11.	B	44.	J
12.	F	45.	A
13.	D	46.	G
14.	G	47.	B
15.	C	48.	G
16.	F	49.	D
17.	A	50.	H
18.	H	51.	D
19.	A	52.	G
20.	J	53.	D
21.	D	54.	F
22.	F	55.	B
23.	C	56.	H
24.	F	57.	A
25.	B	58.	H
26.	G	59.	A
27.	B	60.	F
28.	H	61.	C
29.	D	62.	H
30.	H	63.	C
31.	C	64.	F
32.	J	65.	H
33.	C	66.	B

Unit 1

In this unit you will learn how to

Lesson 1.1	Recognize and Recall Details
Lesson 1.2	Understand Stated Concepts
Lesson 1.3	Draw Conclusions
Lesson 1.4	Summarize and Paraphrase
Lesson 1.5	Identify Cause and Effect
Lesson 1.6	Identify Style Techniques
Lesson 1.7	Find the Main Idea

You will practice the following workplace skills

Lesson 1.1	Locate Details in a Want Ad
Lesson 1.2	Understand Stated Concepts in a Policy
Lesson 1.3	Draw Conclusions from a Time-off Request Form
Lesson 1.4	Summarize and Paraphrase a Procedures Document
Lesson 1.5	Recognize Cause and Effect in a Performance Assessment Form
Lesson 1.6	Understand Style Techniques in E-mails
Lesson 1.7	Recognize Main Idea in an Employee Handbook

You will also learn new words and their meanings and put your reading skills to work in written activities. You will get additional reading practice in *Reading Basics Intermediate 2 Reader*.

Lesson 1.1

Recognize and Recall Details

Every passage has a topic, which is what the passage is about. Details are additional information related to the topic that describe, explain, and clarify. When you read, look for details that tell about the subject. You may not be able to remember every detail in a passage, so you should look at each detail as you read and decide if it relates to the topic in a significant way. If it does not do this, you do not need to remember it.

Recognizing and recalling details is an important part of reading. The details you find will help you understand the topic better and will provide important information. Descriptive details help you picture something, while factual details tell you more about the topic. Thinking about details can help you enjoy the experience of reading more.

> In the Nile River valley, the Egyptians founded an early civilization. Every year the Nile gently flooded the valley, enriching the soil with silt and minerals. This fertile soil meant that the Egyptians could grow a variety of food. Without the Nile, Egypt would have been a dry, barren desert.

The passage above contains descriptive details and factual details. Most of the details are facts that tell how the Nile flooded and made the soil fertile. Look at the last sentence. The words *dry* and *barren* are descriptive. They tell about what the desert would have looked and felt like without the water from the Nile.

Read the passage below. Then underline the details that show why Rhodes's manager thought he was a good hitter. Circle a detail that describes how Rhodes looked or dressed.

> Leo Durocher, the great baseball manager, once said that Dusty Rhodes was the craziest looking ballplayer he had ever seen. He wore his cap at a funny angle, and he stayed out all night when he should have been sleeping. However, Durocher knew that Rhodes could hit. Because he could hit, the New York Giants won the National League pennant in 1954. During the regular season, Rhodes went to bat only 164 times, but he hit 15 home runs and drove in 50 runs.

Did you underline "Rhodes went to bat only 164 times, but he hit 15 home runs and drove in 50 runs"? This detail gives statistics to show that Rhodes was a good hitter. Did you circle "He wore his cap at a funny angle"? This detail is descriptive. It helps the reader picture how Rhodes dressed and why his manager thought he was "the craziest looking ballplayer he had ever seen."

Read each passage. Then write the details that answer each question.

In 14th-century Spain, men wore false beards that were dyed to match their clothes. Beards, or chin wigs, were quite fashionable among Spanish aristocrats. Some men changed their beards as often as they changed their clothes. They might wear a yellow or a crimson beard during the day and change into a long black beard to go to a formal party at night.

1. In what century were false beards popular?

_____

2. What was another name for the beards?

_____

3. What color beards did the men have?

_____

4. Why would men change beards so often?

_____

The beards started to cause problems when some men used them as disguises. People wearing similar beards were often mistaken for one another. Police arrested the wrong bearded men, and villains could escape trouble by changing their beards. Finally rulers outlawed the wearing of false beards.

5. Why were false beards outlawed?

_____

6. Give three details that tell why the beards caused problems.

_____

_____

_____

Read each passage. Then answer the questions.

> Protective coloring helps many animals hide. Colors and patterns help the animals camouflage themselves by blending into the scene. Stripes on tigers make them hard to see in tall grasses. The leopard's spots help disguise the outline of its body, making it harder to pick out in the grass and trees. Many flatfishes change color to match their background. Many arctic animals, including the snowshoe hare and lemming, change from summer brown to winter white.

1. The topic of the passage is that
   A animals' coloring helps them hide to protect themselves.
   B arctic animals change colors to disguise themselves.
   C spots and stripes help animals hunt.
   D animals are better at hiding themselves than people are.

2. Write two details that tell more about the topic.

   _____

   _____

> Adult humans are made of about 66 percent water. It is in blood, inside cells, and in the space between the cells. Water leaves the body through sweat, breath, and waste. Keeping the right amount of water in the body is important. If there is too little, cells shrivel and shrink. If there is too much, they swell like balloons.
>
> Water performs many important functions within the body. It carries food to all the cells, removes waste from the cells, and keeps the body at just the right temperature. While many people can survive a few weeks without food, no one can survive more than a few days without water.

3. Most of the details in the first paragraph
   F explain a fact or an idea.
   G do not relate to the topic.
   H tell a story.
   J give sensory descriptions.

4. Write two details that explain the uses of water in the body.

   _____

Read the passage. Then circle the letter of the answer to each question.

Many words that we use today began as people's names. Charles Macintosh invented a waterproof fabric by cementing two layers of rubber together with a liquid similar to gasoline. Today we sometimes call a raincoat a *mackintosh*. Captain Charles Boycott was a manager of property. His neighbors thought his rents were too high, so they joined together and refused to speak to him. Today, if you refuse to buy something or to spend money at a certain place, you are *boycotting* the business. John Montagu, Earl of Sandwich, asked for a piece of meat between two slices of bread so he could eat quickly while playing cards. He used the bread because he didn't want to get his fingers greasy. Now we use bread and fillings to make *sandwiches*.

1. Most of the details in this passage
   A give reasons for boycotting.
   B describe Macintosh's method of waterproofing.
   C give examples of words made from people's names.
   D tell the story of the history of English.

2. Charles Macintosh cemented two layers of rubber together with
   F water.
   G pine sap.
   H glue.
   J a liquid similar to gasoline.

3. Charles Macintosh's fabric
   A was woven from wool.
   B was purely decorative.
   C was a fire repellant.
   D was waterproof.

4. Captain Charles Boycott was
   F a manager of property.
   G a bill collector.
   H a store owner.
   J a bank manager.

5. The neighbors of Captain Charles Boycott
   A refused to talk with him.
   B thought he was rude.
   C paid rent willingly.
   D made him leave town.

6. The Earl of Sandwich invented sandwiches
   F in the kitchen.
   G during a card game.
   H during a lecture.
   J for a late night snack.

7. The first sandwich was made from
   A bread and eggs.
   B a piece of meat between two slices of bread.
   C a bagel and cheese.
   D an English muffin and meat.

8. John Montagu created a sandwich
   F to use up his bread.
   G so he could eat quickly.
   H because steak was too costly.
   J to start a new trend.

Workplace Skill: Locate Details in a Want Ad

Help wanted ads provide information about job openings. You can find want ads in newspapers or online. To understand want ads, you need to pay attention to the details that provide additional information related to the job. You need to be able to understand the details and abbreviations in a want ad to assess the qualifications and skills you need for a particular job.

Read the ad below. Then circle the letter of the answer to each question.

DENTAL ASSISTANT

New dental practice seeks licensed assistant. F/T 8–4, Tues.–Sat. Medical, Dental, and Paid Vacation. Looking for person with high standards and sense of humor. Competitive salary. Send résumé to: Dr. Abba Achebe, 19 Oak Street, Sycamore, NH 83025 or e-mail at dhiggins@reachme.com   EOE

---

1. Which benefits are offered in the ad?

   A   Saturdays and holidays off

   B   credits toward a dental license

   C   medical and dental benefits

   D   college tuition reimbursement

2. According to the details in the ad, what do you know about Dr. Achebe?

   F   Dr. Achebe is difficult to work with.

   G   Dr. Achebe does not pay a good salary.

   H   Dr. Achebe is opening a new practice.

   J   Dr. Achebe is a practical joker.

3. What is the abbreviation for equal opportunity employer?

   A   Equop

   B   EOE

   C   EOA

   D   OpEm

4. What is the abbreviation for full time?

   F   FLTM

   G   P/T

   H   F/T

   J   FM

Write the answer to each question.

5. According to the details in the ad, what type of person is Dr. Achebe looking for in a dental assistant?

   _____

   _____

6. According to the details in the ad, what should you do if you were interested in applying for this position?

   _____

   _____

Write for Work

Reread the want ad on page 18. In a notebook, write a letter to Dr. Achebe, explaining why you are interested in the position. State the main idea of the ad in your letter. Include at least three details from the ad.

 Reading Extension

Turn to "King Kong" on page 1 of *Reading Basics Intermediate 2 Reader*. After you have read and/or listened to the article, answer the questions below.

Circle the letter of the answer to each question.

1. What building does Kong climb in the original film?
   A   the World Trade Center
   B   the Empire State Building
   C   the Sears Tower
   D   the Chrysler Building

2. How long did it take to make *King Kong*?
   F   three months
   G   six months
   H   one year
   J   two years

3. Most of the budget on *King Kong* went to
   A   actors' salaries.
   B   travel expenses.
   C   the cost of caring for the animals.
   D   special effects.

4. What fairy tale does the author compare to *King Kong*?
   F   *Cinderella*
   G   *Hansel and Gretel*
   H   *Rumpelstiltskin*
   J   *Beauty and the Beast*

Write the answer to each question.

5. Why were the people models made with metal joints?

   _____

   _____

   _____

6. Name two of the sympathetic ape movies that followed the original *King Kong*.

   _____

   _____

   _____

Explore Words

Two vowels can come together and stand for one long vowel sound. For example, *ai* stands for the long *a* sound in *mailbox*. Look at these other vowel combinations:

long *a*   *ai, ay*   long *e*   *ea, ee, ie*   long *i*   *ie*

long *o*   *oa, oe, ow*   long *u*   *ue*

Read the sentences below. Circle the word in each sentence that has the same vowel sound as the underlined word. The first item has been done for you.

1. (Please) keep this information to yourself.

2. Joe's son scored a goal in soccer the other day.

3. These books are due back on the first of June.

4. I am seeing my trainer every Monday this month.

5. Nuri will visit Joan when he goes to Maine.

6. May the baby have a slice of blueberry pie?

COMPOUND WORDS

A compound word is made of two smaller words. You can often use the smaller words to figure out the meaning of a compound word. For example, *steamboat* is a compound word made of the words *steam* and *boat*. A steamboat is a boat powered by steam.

Match the compound word with its meaning. Then write the letter on the line.

_____ **1.** basketball

_____ **2.** armchair

_____ **3.** bathroom

_____ **4.** daydream

a. a dream you have during the day

b. the room where you can take a bath

c. a chair that has arms

d. a ball to throw through a basket

SYNONYMS

Synonyms are words that have the same or almost the same meaning. For example, *nervous* and *worried* are synonyms.

Find the synonym in the box for each numbered word. Write the word on the line.

tiny	sleepy	glad	dull	silly	end

1. happy   _____

2. boring   _____

3. little   _____

4. foolish   _____

5. finish   _____

6. tired   _____

A prefix is a word part that can be added to the beginning of a word. Adding prefixes to words changes the meanings of the words.

pre- means "before"   *re-* means "again"   *sub-* means "under"

Add a prefix to each word in the right column to make it match the meaning. Write the new word on the line.

1. play again _____ play

2. before dawn _____ dawn

3. discover again _____ discover

4. below the basement _____ basement

5. pay before _____ pay

6. rinse before _____ rinse

7. below the tropics _____ tropical

8. build again _____ build

9. before the sale _____ sale

ACADEMIC VOCABULARY

Knowing these high-frequency words will help you in many school subjects.

detail   an individual feature, fact, or item

subject   what a certain text is about

recall   to remember

passage   a piece of writing

clarify   to make clear; explain

Complete the sentences below using one of the words above.

1. What was the _____ of the lecture?

2. Asura didn't understand the directions. She asked her boss to _____ them.

3. Carlotta read the _____ carefully.

4. The party was perfect, down to the last _____.

5. Rui could not _____ where she had seen the man before.

Lesson 1.2

Understand Stated Concepts

When you read, it is important to understand the ideas and concepts presented in the text. Sometimes a selection will give new information, and sometimes an unfamiliar idea will be explained or an unfamiliar word will be defined. You may need to read a passage more than once to understand the information that is presented.

Some of the ideas in a passage will be stated directly, while others will be implied. It is important to distinguish between stated and unstated concepts. Knowing which ideas were directly stated will help you understand what you have read. It will also help you distinguish which ideas came from the text and which you inferred based on the text and your own opinions. Read the example below and identify stated concepts:

> Many roundworms are parasites, meaning they live inside the body of a larger animal and feed off it. Examples include hookworms and eyeworms. They cause diseases in livestock and in humans.

There are concepts that are stated directly and concepts that are implied. It is directly stated that hookworms and eyeworms are parasites. The writer also directly states that parasites live inside the body of a larger animal. The idea that roundworm parasites hurt people and animals is stated indirectly. The reader can infer it by reading the stated concepts that the parasites cause disease and feed off people and animals.

Read the passage. Underline the sentences that state how sand fleas got their name. Circle the sentence that states what kind of creature sand fleas are.

> Have you ever disturbed a mass of tangled seaweed that the tide has left high and dry on the beach? If so, you probably exposed a colony of tiny, bouncing creatures. Although they are commonly referred to as sand fleas, the animals are not insects. They are crustaceans. Their name comes from their habit of leaping into the air as fleas do. The fleas come out at night to look for food. During the day, they like to stay safely buried in the sand.

Did you underline "Their name comes from their habit of leaping into the air as fleas do," and "During the day, they like to stay safely buried in the sand"? These sentences tell why the creatures are called sand fleas.

You should have circled "They are crustaceans." This sentence directly states the kind of creature that sand fleas are.

Read the passage. Then circle *true* or *false* for each statement. If the answer is false, explain why using concepts stated in the passage.

Ocean thermal energy conversion, or OTEC, is a way of changing the ocean's heat into energy that can be used to run an engine. The water that covers almost 75 percent of the surface of the Earth absorbs an enormous amount of solar heat. French inventor Georges Claude built the first OTEC power plant in Cuba in 1930 intending to make use of the heat. The plant was unsuccessful, but researchers around the world have recently begun to experiment with ocean heat again. The U.S. Department of Energy built an OTEC test site on board a U.S. Navy tanker.

1. Ocean thermal energy conversion is a way to heat the ocean's water.

true   false

_____

2. The water that covers much of the surface of the Earth takes in solar heat.

true   false

_____

3. OTEC was first developed in the 1960s.

true   false

_____

4. Georges Claude built the first OTEC power plant on a U.S. Navy tanker.

true   false

_____

5. The first plant was a great success.

true   false

_____

6. OTEC may offer a solution to the energy crisis.

true   false

_____

Read each passage. Then write three important facts from each passage on the lines.

> Maxwell Montes is one of the tallest mountain ranges in the solar system. It is more than a mile higher than Mount Everest. Located on Venus, Maxwell Montes towers more than 35,000 feet above the planet's plain level. No one has actually seen this mountain range close up, but Earth-based radar instruments suggest that the slopes of Maxwell have an extremely rocky surface. The mountain range has a large crater named Cleopatra on its eastern margin. Cleopatra is an impact crater. Impact craters form when objects floating in space strike the surface of a planet or moon.

1. _____

2. _____

3. _____

> Tasmanian devils live primarily on the island of Tasmania, off the coast of Australia. When another animal or a human threatens a Tasmanian devil, it will throw a wild temper tantrum. It will bare its sharp teeth, growl, and lunge. People saw these rowdy fits and named the animals "devils." However, being threatened isn't the only reason the devils will fly into a rage. When fighting for a mate or defending their food, the devils will behave in a similarly ill-tempered manner.

4. _____

5. _____

6. _____

> A nor'easter is a particularly strong windstorm that moves north up the Atlantic coast. These storms can create intense winds and rains as well as heavy snow and large waves. There have been a number of nor'easters famous for severe damage from wind and snow.

7. _____

8. _____

9. _____

Read the passage. Then circle the letter of the answer to each question.

What we see around us does not simply flow through our eyes right into our minds. The eye is one of the most complicated and delicate instruments in nature. At the back of the eye is a kind of curved screen called the retina. The retina receives two-dimensional images from outside. These flat images offer information about color, size, and shadow, but it is the overlapping of the two slightly different images— one from each eye—that gives the outside world a three-dimensional look. This superimposition of images takes place in the brain. Without the combining of the two images, the world outside would look flat.

1. What does the writer call "one of the most complicated and delicate instruments in nature"?
   A the retina
   B the curved screen
   C the eye
   D the eyelid

2. Where is the retina located?
   F at the back of the eye
   G on the surface of the eye
   H in the brain
   J in the eyelid

3. What is the retina?
   A the brain
   B a kind of curved screen
   C a bone
   D a picture

4. Describe the two-dimensional images that the retina receives.
   F large
   G curved
   H flat
   J shallow

5. What do the two-dimensional images show?
   A overlapping
   B three-dimensional images
   C x-rays
   D color, size, and shadow

6. What does *superimposition* mean?
   F perception
   G overlapping
   H dimension
   J detection

7. Where does superimposition happen?
   A in the brain
   B in the eye
   C in the retina
   D in the nose

8. What does superimposition do?
   F makes the images appear flat
   G receives two-dimensional images
   H makes the images appear three-dimensional
   J changes color perceptions

Workplace Skill:
Understand Stated Concepts in a Policy

Companies create policies so that employees know what is expected of them in the workplace. Often these concepts are directly stated in titles, headings, and topic sentences. Details support the concepts by giving more information about them. Using details to help you understand concepts that are not directly stated can help you better understand what you read.

Read the policy. Then circle the letter of the answer to each question.

Arco Office Supply
Internet and E-mail Policy

Internet and e-mail access on employees' computers is to be used only to perform duties directly related to company business. If your job requires Internet and e-mail access, this capability will be installed on your computer. Only approved employees will have Internet and e-mail access.

During paid work hours, the Internet is only to be used for company business. This policy is to protect company information. Internet use opens the door to corrupting our system with viruses. For this reason, we ask that the Internet be used only as needed.

You are paid to perform your job duties, which means you should not be using company time or property for personal business. Employees who violate this policy are subject to disciplinary action, up to and including termination.

Like the Internet, e-mail is to be used exclusively for conducting company business. Private company business should not be sent or discussed outside of the company. Personal e-mails and personal business should not be handled using the company computer or e-mail. Sending noncompany e-mails will lead to disciplinary action.

1. Which idea is directly stated in the first paragraph?

   A   All employees will be able to use the Internet.

   B   All computers will have Internet access.

   C   Internet access is only for work-related duties.

   D   All jobs require Internet access.

2. Which idea is implied in the third paragraph?

   F   Using the company Internet for personal use is like stealing from the company.

   G   Using the company Internet for personal use is okay if you get all your work done.

   H   Only management and IT leaders can use company Internet for personal use.

   J   Viruses are the main problem caused by using the company Internet for personal use.

Write for Work

Imagine that an employee you are supervising is using the Internet for personal use during office hours. You have decided to handle the problem by writing a general e-mail. In your e-mail, remind all employees of the company policy and give three reasons employees should not use the Internet during work hours. Write the e-mail in a notebook.

  Reading Extension

Turn to "Nightmare on Chemical Street: The Love Canal Story" on page 10 of *Reading Basics Intermediate 2 Reader*. After you have read and/or listened to the article, answer the questions below.

Circle the letter of the answer to each question.

1. Why did William T. Love stop building the canal?
   - **A** The canal was finished.
   - **B** He ran out of money.
   - **C** There was no longer a need for a canal.
   - **D** He wanted to build a school on the land.

2. What health problems did Barbara Quimby experience in her twenties?
   - **F** She had kidney and lung problems.
   - **G** She had a hernia and an ulcer.
   - **H** She developed a strange rash and lightheadedness.
   - **J** She had cancer.

3. Why weren't the chemicals removed from Love Canal?
   - **A** The school was closed, so it didn't matter.
   - **B** The government ran out of money.
   - **C** They no longer posed a threat.
   - **D** They were too dangerous to handle.

Write the answer to each question.

4. Why were some residents afraid to have children?

   _____

5. Why was Lois Gibbs concerned when she learned that her son's school was built on a chemical dump?

   _____

Explore Words

CONSONANT BLENDS

The consonants *s, l, r,* and *n* can blend with other consonants. These words have two-letter blends: *brim, sleep, skin, risk, tent,* and *band.* These words have three-letter blends: *scream, shrug,* and *three.* When you see a consonant blend, say the sound of each consonant. Remember that consonant pairs *ch, sh,* and *th* stand for one sound.

Write a consonant blend on the line to make a word in each sentence.

1. Keyon _____ugged and said he didn't know. *(thr, shr, scr)*

2. Her husba_____ will pick her up after work. *(nd, nt, sk)*

3. Mai was abse_____ because she didn't feel well. *(nd, nt, sk)*

4. I had to _____ing her kids to day care. *(sl, br, sk)*

5. Don't let that cat _____atch you! *(sk, scr, thr)*

6. We try to be _____ifty to save money. *(thr, scr, shr)*

SPELLING: PLURALS

Plural means "more than one." To make most words plural, add *-s* to the end of the word (*student/students*). To form the plural of words that end with *s, ss, sh, x,* or *ch,* add *-es* (*boss/bosses*). For words that end in *y,* change the *y* to *i* and add *-es* (*penny/pennies*).

Write the plural of each word on the line next to it.

1. lady _____   4. desk _____

2. branch _____   5. bus _____

3. hairbrush _____   6. box _____

ANTONYMS

Antonyms are words that have the opposite or almost the opposite meanings. For example, the words *remember* and *forget* are antonyms.

Circle the word in each row that is an antonym for the first word.

1. low	easy	high	down
2. question	answer	letter	ask
3. plain	boring	dull	fancy
4. true	correct	false	exact

Reading Basics · Intermediate 2

CONTEXT CLUES

If a sentence includes a word that you do not know, look for context clues. Context clues are other words in the sentence or in the sentences around it that help you figure out the meaning of the unknown word. Look at this sentence: *Because Dawud is underlined perpetually late, we always have to wait for him.* Context clues help you guess that *perpetually* means "always."

Use context clues to help you understand the meaning of the underlined word. Write the meaning of the word.

1. We heard the cows bellow. Their cries woke us up. _____

2. The bold horse ran up the hill. The others followed their brave leader. _____

3. The rafting trip was hazardous. No one had told me it would be so dangerous. _____

4. There will soon be festivities. The celebrations will start when the guests arrive. _____

5. Drenched by the rainstorm, we changed our soaked clothes. _____

6. I knew that the fever made me look flushed. I could feel my face turn red. _____

ACADEMIC VOCABULARY

Knowing these high-frequency words will help you in many school subjects.

distinguish	to perceive or recognize
imply	to strongly suggest something
directly	in a clear way
state	to say or tell
infer	to decide or conclude something from evidence and reasoning rather than from direct statements

Complete the sentences below using one of the words above.

1. The lawyer asked the witness to _____ only the facts.

2. From the broken bottles, dirty plates, and general mess, Danielle could _____ that there had been a party the night before.

3. The puppies all had different collars to help _____ them from one another.

4. Juan didn't ask Carla out, but he did _____ that he would like a date.

5. Then Carla asked him _____ if he'd like to go to the movies on Friday.

Lesson 1.3

Draw Conclusions

A conclusion is a decision or opinion you form based on something you read or hear. Drawing a conclusion requires you to think about what is stated in addition to using your own experiences. Drawing a conclusion tests your ability to reason.

Drawing a conclusion might be understood as putting information together as follows:

stated facts + implied ideas + personal experience and knowledge = conclusion

More than one conclusion may be drawn from a fact or a given set of facts, so it is important to make sure that the conclusion you draw is valid. Examine the stated facts and implied ideas to ensure that they are true and that you understand them. Then think about the personal knowledge and experience you applied and make sure it is appropriate to the situation. Finally, look at the conclusion you have drawn to make sure it is a natural outcome of all the facts you examined. Read these sentences:

Sometimes hiccups are so violent or long-lasting that medical help is necessary. In most cases, however, they stop quickly with no side effects.

What conclusion did you draw? Think about what ideas are implied and your own experience of having hiccups. One valid conclusion is that while some hiccups are serious, they are usually not a big deal.

Read the passage. What conclusion might you draw about how the Chinese people felt about Qin Shihuangdi? What facts, implied ideas, and personal knowledge help you to determine whether it is a valid conclusion?

The Qin dynasty in China began in 221 B.C. Qin Shihuangdi declared himself the first emperor. During his reign, he accomplished many important things, including developing a bureaucratic government to organize the state. He standardized laws, the written language, and weights and measures. He ordered a network of canals and roads to be built. He also linked forts that formed the Great Wall of China. However, his harsh treatment of the people led to a revolt.

One conclusion might be that the people were happy about the accomplishments that Qin Shihuangdi brought about because these things likely improved their lives. However, the passage also includes the fact that he treated the people harshly, which caused them to revolt. This information, along with the knowledge that no one likes to be treated poorly, leads to the conclusion that the people also resented Qin Shihuangdi for his harsh treatment of them.

Read the passage. Then write the conclusion that could be drawn from each set of facts, implied ideas, and knowledge.

There are several reasons that earthquakes occur. One cause is rock sliding along a crack, or fault, in Earth's crust. The sliding rock causes vibrations that move through the ground like waves through water. These "seismic waves" cause some areas to rise and others to fall. Cities are most affected when the waves cause buildings to collapse. Flexible buildings can move with these waves because they bend with them like trees bending in the wind. Rigid buildings are stiff like dead branches and do not bend. Buildings sitting on solid rock tend to move with the rock. They ride the waves like a surfer on a surfboard, and the rock absorbs some of the shock. Buildings standing on loose earth shake more violently than those on solid rock.

1. **Fact:** Flexible buildings can bend with seismic waves, like trees bending in the wind.

   Implied Idea: During an earthquake, flexible buildings are less likely to collapse.

   Knowledge: Architects are responsible for designing safe structures.

   Conclusion: _____

   _____

2. **Fact:** Rigid buildings are stiff like dead branches and do not bend.

   Implied Idea: During an earthquake, rigid buildings are more likely to collapse.

   Knowledge: Earthquakes cause more damage to some buildings than to others.

   Conclusion: _____

   _____

3. **Fact:** Buildings sitting on solid rock move with the rock, which absorbs some of the shock.

   Implied Idea: During an earthquake, buildings on rock are less likely to be damaged than those on loose earth.

   Knowledge: Something built on a flat, solid surface is more likely to remain standing versus something built on softer ground, like a sandy beach.

   Conclusion: _____

   _____

Read each passage. Then write the answer to each question.

Time capsules are not pills. They are containers that are filled with souvenirs and often buried under special places or sealed into the corners of buildings. One capsule was buried in 1938 under the site of the New York World's Fair. It is long and thin like a torpedo and made of metal. The capsule contains a microfilm of 20th-century knowledge, images and film of famous people and events, a Bible, a toothbrush, and even women's makeup. Full of memories and history, time capsules are made to communicate with people in the distant future.

1. You can conclude that time capsules are not meant to be opened for many years because

_____

2. What stated facts and implied ideas helped you draw this conclusion?

_____

3. What personal experiences helped you draw this conclusion?

_____

Long ago there were no yardsticks, rulers, or tape measures. When people first began to measure things, they probably used their own fingers or hands. They also used their arms and feet. "This is a three-finger spearhead," a person might have said, or "This fish is as long as my foot put down two times." When people measured things in that way, they were using their fingers and feet just as we use inch and foot markings on a yardstick.

4. If people with different-sized feet measured the same thing in "feet," the results would be

_____

5. What stated facts and implied ideas helped you draw this conclusion?

_____

6. What personal experiences helped you draw this conclusion?

_____

Read each passage. Then circle the letter of the answer that completes each statement.

Some people call it the tiger of the sea, but most call it the barracuda. Fast and equipped with razor-sharp teeth and powerful jaws, this fish is one of the most dangerous creatures on Earth. It feeds mostly on smaller fish, but it does attack humans. Naturalists have observed a shrewd hunting style in the barracuda. It waits unnoticed for its prey to swim by, and then it suddenly pounces.

1. You can conclude that the barracuda

A is dangerous only to smaller fish.

B is especially dangerous because it uses surprise attack.

C should be easy to hunt.

D is not as fierce as people think.

People in England have been burning a material very much like dirt for centuries. The substance is known as *peat*, a vegetable matter that has decayed in moist earth. Peat is dug out of the ground, shaped into bricks, and dried. Then it is burned like firewood. The formation of peat is the first step in the creation of coal. Millions of years ago, as landmasses formed, vegetable deposits were buried at various depths in the ground. Deposits that were buried deeply were subject to great pressure and formed coal, while those that remained close to the surface formed peat.

2. You can conclude that

F peat is actually dirt.

G if peat is put under great pressure for a long time, it will turn into coal.

H peat smells like vegetables when it burns.

J peat burns better than wood.

The nomads of the Sahara Desert are always traveling. Water is scarce in the desert, so the nomads move from one freshwater supply to another. One place where water can be found in the desert is an oasis. The Sahara, which is in northern Africa, is the size of the United States, and it has only 90 oases. The area around an oasis has trees and grasses on which the nomads' goats and camels graze. Nomads camp at an oasis until their animals have eaten most of the plants. Then they pack up and move on.

3. You can conclude that a nomad's life

A is very long.

B takes place within a small area.

C is one of wealth and riches.

D means traveling in order to survive.

Workplace Skill: Draw Conclusions from a Time-off Request Form

Forms ask you to fill in information and provide space for you to write or type the information. Forms have a specific function, or purpose—to provide required information in a certain format. Sometimes the questions are clearly stated. Other times you need to come to a conclusion about the kinds of information required.

Read the form. Then circle the letter of the answer to each question below the box.

Time-off Request Form

Employee Information

Name: Date:

Number of Days Requested:

Starting On: Ending On:

Type of Request

☐ Vacation   ☐ Military Leave

☐ Personal Leave   ☐ Family and Medical Leave

☐ Bereavement Leave   ☐ Sick Time

☐ Jury Duty   ☐ Other

I understand that if I am requesting more than 5 consecutive days off, I need to give my manager at least one month's notice prior to the time off.

Comments

_____

_____

Employee Signature

I understand that time away from work is subject to management approval and company policies.

Employee Signature: _____ **Date:** _____

Approved: ☐ YES   ☐ NO

Supervisor/Manager Signature: _____ **Date:** _____

---

1. Gina Savage wants to take time off from September 1 to September 15. What does she need to do?

   A give her manager one month's prior notice

   B give her manager one week's prior notice

   C look through the employee handbook

   D submit the form without signing it

2. Gina's request for time off was denied. What reason might account for this denial?

   F She signed and dated the time off request form.

   G Her request for time off was submitted less than a week prior to the leave days requested.

   H Her supervisor/manager signed the request form.

   J Her request was for bereavement leave.

Write for Work

Imagine you are an employee who needs to submit the Time-off Request Form on page 34 to request time off for a specific reason. In a notebook, write the required information you will need to complete this form.

 **Reading Extension**

Turn to "An Encounter in New Guinea" on page 19 of *Reading Basics Intermediate 2 Reader*. After you have read and/or listened to the article, answer the questions below.

Circle the letter of the answer to each question.

1. The Australian Department of Air and the Royal Australian Air Force both offered an explanation of what Gill had seen. What conclusion can you draw from this?

   A They think the sighting is very important.

   B They do not want to see a UFO.

   C They do not believe Gill saw a UFO.

   D They think Gill saw a UFO.

2. Gill says the aliens mimicked his movements. What conclusion can you draw from this?

   F He thinks there was no one aboard the UFO.

   G He thinks the aliens saw him.

   H He thinks the aliens did not want him to go inside.

   J He thinks the aliens could not land their ship.

Write the answer to each question.

3. Gill thought he had seen a mother ship. What conclusion can you draw about Gill's idea of the possibility of other aliens near Earth?

   _____

   _____

4. The passage states that Gill had researched UFOs before his encounter. What can you conclude from this statement?

   _____

   _____

   _____

Explore Words

When the letter *y* comes at the end of a word, it serves as a vowel and usually stands for the long *e* sound, as in *family*. Final *y* can also stand for the long *i* sound, as in *cry*.

Say each word. If the final *y* stands for the long *e* sound, write *E* on the line. If it stands for the long *i* sound, write *I*.

1. shy _____

2. quickly _____

3. strawberry _____

4. my _____

5. ability _____

6. simplify _____

SYLLABLES

A syllable is a word or word part that has one vowel sound. In closed syllables, the vowel usually stands for its short sound (*it*, *rib*). In silent *e* and open syllables, the vowel usually stands for its long sound (*no*, *note*).

Match each syllable in the left column with a syllable in the right column to form a word. Write the word on the line. Then circle the first syllable if it has a long vowel sound.

1. ro   **a.** ken   _____

2. wag   **b.** dent   _____

3. pine   **c.** on   _____

4. to   **d.** cone   _____

SUFFIXES *-ness, -ment*

A suffix is a word part that can be added to the end of words. Adding a suffix changes the meaning of the word. The suffix *-ness* means "the state of being." The suffix *-ment* means "the result of." *Sickness* means "the state of being sick." *Movement* means "the result of moving."

Add the suffix *-ness* or *-ment* to each base word to make a word that has the meaning shown. Write the new word on the line.

1. sweet_____ means "the state of being sweet" _____

2. enjoy_____ means "the result of enjoying" _____

3. pay_____ means "the result of paying" _____

4. dark_____ means "the state of being dark" _____

SPELLING: BASE WORDS AND ENDINGS

You can add the endings -ed and -ing to the end of base words. When you add these endings, remember these spelling rules:

- When a word ends with silent e, drop the e. Then add -ed or -ing.

  bake   baked   baking

- When a word ends in a consonant followed by y, change the y to i. Then add -ed. Do not change the spelling to add -ing.

  carry   carried   carrying

- When a one-syllable word with one vowel ends in a single consonant, double the consonant. Then add -ed or -ing.

  zip   zipped   zipping

Add the ending to each word. Write the new word on the line.

1. regret + ed   _____

2. invent + ing   _____

3. supply + ed   _____

4. simplify + ing   _____

5. cry + ed   _____

6. decide + ing   _____

7. replace + ed   _____

8. visit + ing   _____

ACADEMIC VOCABULARY

Knowing these high-frequency words will help you in many school subjects.

conclusion   a judgment or decision made after considering information

draw   to obtain something from

valid   supporting the intended point or claim

appropriate   proper in the circumstances

always   at all times

Complete the sentences below using one of the words above.

1. Irina tried to _____ inspiration from the ocean.

2. The light turned green to show that Karim's code was _____.

3. Emilio jumped to a _____ without thinking carefully about the facts.

4. It is not _____ to wear a ball gown to play basketball.

5. Gretchen _____ seemed to be talking, even when she was supposed to be quiet.

Lesson 1.4

Summarize and Paraphrase

A summary is a brief retelling of the most important ideas in a passage. When you summarize, first identify the main idea. Then decide which details are important enough to include. Most details can be left out. Someone who has not read the original passage should be able to understand it by reading your summary.

When you paraphrase, think about what each sentence or group of sentences means and then restate them using words that you understand well. Make sure that your paraphrase does not change the meaning of the writer's original ideas. Unlike a summary, a paraphrase includes most of the details in the original passage.

> The Mexican government gave grants of land to American settlers in its province of Texas during the 1820s. Later, these settlers revolted against Mexico. They declared Texas an independent republic in 1836. The brief but fierce war was famous for the battle of the Alamo in San Antonio.

A good summary of this passage is, *American settlers received land grants from Mexico and later fought a war to become their own state of Texas.* The summary leaves out many details but includes the main idea.

A paraphrase of the passage is, *In the 1820s American settlers received land grants in the province of Texas. In 1836 the settlers revolted against Mexico and decided to become their own state. The battle of the Alamo is a famous battle during the short war.*

Read the passage. Decide whether the sentence that follows is a summary or a paraphrase.

The frogfish, which lives near the bottom of the ocean, uses the tentacle that grows out of its head to catch other fish. This tentacle is called a "longlure" and resembles a fishing pole. The frogfish lies in wait with its fleshy "bait" floating in the water. Small fish mistake the lure for food and swim close to the lure. They are captured, and the crafty frogfish immediately gobbles them up.

The frogfish captures and eats smaller fish using a special tentacle that floats in the water and looks like bait.

This is a summary. It includes the main idea, which is how the frogfish catches small fish to eat. It also includes the important detail about the frogfish's unusual tentacle. A paraphrase would have included information about the tentacle looking like a fishing pole and small fish mistaking the lure for food.

Read each passage. Then circle the letter of the answer to each question.

Although at its surface ocean water appears to be blue or green, in its depths it is pitch black. Color is the result of reflected light, and on the ocean's surface, the various living organisms in the water reflect sunlight. They absorb some of the light and reflect the rest. If the water appears green, it is because green light is being reflected by the plants and minerals in the water. At the depth of 3,000 feet, all the light has been absorbed by the organisms above. What keeps the fish from bumping into one another in the dark? Some sense objects by sonar, which is a way of bouncing sounds off objects. Other fish that live very deep in the ocean have the ability to actually give off their own light.

1. Which of these statements best summarizes the passage?
   A   Light in the ocean is colored by the plants and animals in the water. They reflect sunlight. In places where the light does not penetrate, the ocean is pitch black.
   B   Some fish that live deep in the ocean give off their own light. It is important because at the depth where they live, no light penetrates.
   C   There is no color in the depths of the ocean because there is no light. The animals in the water above soak it all up.
   D   The ocean appears to have different colors. The plants and animals in it absorb the sunlight. This is why the ocean looks blue and green.

A frog has no ribs, and its chest does not expand and contract when it breathes. Unlike most air-breathing animals, the frog swallows air into its lungs rather than inhaling it. For this reason, it is not necessary for the frog to hold its breath when it jumps into water. All the frog has to do is stop swallowing air. A frog can live for hours without breathing because it gets part of its oxygen supply through its skin. In very cold weather, a frog will sink to the bottom of a pond and can remain there indefinitely. Its breathing movements stop, and the blood circulating through its skin absorbs enough oxygen from the water to sustain life.

2. Which of these statements is a paraphrase of the last two sentences of the passage?
   F   A frog has no ribs, and its chest does not move when it breathes. It swallows air in a gulping fashion and sinks to the bottom of a pond in the winter.
   G   In cold weather frogs stay on the bottom of ponds and absorb oxygen through their skin. The circulation of their blood helps them absorb enough oxygen to survive for a long time.
   H   Frogs can survive for long periods in cold weather by staying underwater.
   J   Frogs get oxygen through their skin and by swallowing air.

Write a summary of the passage. Then paraphrase the first three sentences.

> The Dead Sea is an inland lake located between Israel and Jordan. Lying 1,312 feet below sea level, it is the lowest body of water on Earth's surface. The salt content of the water in the Dead Sea is about 30 percent, whereas the salt content of seawater is about 3.5 percent. Even though freshwater from the Jordan River flows into the Dead Sea, the water evaporates in the extreme heat. A person can float on the surface of the water with ease. It is almost impossible to sink because saltwater has a higher relative density (weight) than freshwater. Therefore, a person is actually lighter in saltwater than in freshwater.

Summary

1. _____

_____

Paraphrase

2. _____

_____

_____

_____

Write a paraphrase of the passage.

> Every living cell has its own purpose. The first purpose of every cell is to survive. If any part of the cell fails, the entire cell will die. The tiny parts inside each cell must be organized for survival. Different cells are organized for different purposes depending on cell's role within an organism.

3. _____

_____

_____

_____

_____

Circle the letter of the best summary and the best paraphrase for each passage.

> Neither land mammals nor people of any kind are native to the land in the Antarctic Circle. The only human beings living at the South Pole are scientists who are studying the area. Penguins and several other seabirds compose much of the wildlife found in this icebound region. The only important mammalian life in the Antarctic is the marine form. Some seals and a few whales live at the South Pole all year round. The absence of land animals is one of the striking features of Antarctica.

1. Summary

A   The Antarctic is different from other areas on Earth.

B   Seabirds and marine mammals are the only native animals in Antarctica.

2. Paraphrase

F   No land mammals are native to the Antarctic Circle. No people live there either, except for scientists. The only mammals—seals and whales—are marine mammals that live in the water. Penguins and other seabirds also live there. The absence of land animals is a feature of the continent.

G   No animals live at the South Pole. The only humans are scientists. Some marine mammals—seals and whales—live in the water. Having no animals is one of the features of this area.

> It is a common but false belief that porcupines shoot their quills at an enemy when attacked. The truth is that the quills stand upright when the animal is disturbed. This is much like what a cat's fur does when the cat senses danger. The porcupine's quills are loosely attached to its body and tail and come out upon the slightest contact with other objects. When attacked, the porcupine thrashes about actively with its tail. If the tail comes into contact with anything, its quills are likely to become detached.

3. Summary

A   Porcupines do not shoot quills at their enemies. When they are frightened, their quills stand up, and they thrash their tails, leaving quills behind.

B   Porcupines have an intriguing defense system. Their quills act like a cat's fur, standing up when they are scared. Their quills easily get detached if they come into contact with other objects.

4. Paraphrase

F   Porcupines do not shoot quills. When disturbed, the porcupine's quills stand upright. The porcupine thrashes its tail. The quills come out.

G   It is a false belief that porcupines shoot their quills. The quills stand upright when the porcupine is in danger. The quills are loosely attached and come out easily. When attacked, the porcupine thrashes its tail. Quills may come out if the tail touches something.

Workplace Skill: Summarize and Paraphrase a Procedures Document

Company procedures tell an employee how to do something. There may be occasions when you need to summarize or paraphrase this information. When you summarize, you briefly retell the main idea and the most important details. When you paraphrase, you retell all of the information in your own words.

Read the procedures document. Then circle the letter of the answer to each question.

Internal Transfer Procedure

Springhouse Care Center has an internal job posting. This posting informs employees about open positions before they are advertised to the public. The posting will go up each Friday morning on the information board. To apply for an open position:

Step 1: Make sure you meet these requirements:

- You are a current full-time or part-time employee.
- You have held your position for six months and have your supervisor's permission to apply.
- You meet the qualifications listed for the position for which you are applying.

Step 2: Complete an internal transfer form:

- Get an internal transfer form from Human Resources and fill out the form completely. If you have a résumé, you may attach a copy to your form.
- Have your current supervisor sign your internal transfer form.

Step 3: Submit your completed and signed form to Human Resources by the deadline.

Step 4: Candidates who are qualified for an open position will be contacted for an interview with the hiring manager. First preference will be given to current employees, but we do not guarantee that open positions will go to internal candidates. We reserve the right to interview and hire the most qualified candidates for all openings.

1. Which sentence best summarizes Step 2?

   A Don't forget to have your supervisor sign your form.

   B You can attach a résumé to your internal transfer form.

   C Internal transfer forms are available in the Human Resources department.

   D Fill out the internal transfer form and have your supervisor sign it.

2. Which sentence is the best paraphrase of the first sentence from Step 4?

   F A supervisor will contact candidates who have the right skills and experience.

   G All candidates will be contacted by a supervisor for an interview.

   H Open positions will be filled by candidates who are qualified for an interview.

   J A qualified supervisor will be contacted to interview candidates.

Write for Work

Imagine you work for Springhouse Care Center and you see a position on the internal job posting for which you want to apply. In a notebook, summarize the steps listed on page 42 that you would follow to apply for the position.

 Reading Extension

Turn to "Ocean-born Mary" on page 26 of *Reading Basics Intermediate 2 Reader*. After you have read and/or listened to the article, answer the questions below.

Circle the letter of the answer to each question.

1. Choose the best summary for paragraph 4.

   A The captain didn't know what to do. The other ship raised the skull and crossbones. The members of the other ship had swords and pistols. They captured the passengers of the immigrant ship.

   B Pirates, led by a man named Pedro, captured the immigrant ship.

   C Pirates captured the immigrant ship.

   D The captain knew his ship was an easy target. The pirates were able to capture the ship. A man named Pedro was in charge.

2. Choose the best paraphrase for the first two sentences of paragraph 12.

   F Not all of the story is based on fact.

   G Some of the story is true, and some of it is legend.

   H The story up to this point can be proven by facts. The legend is what you're about to read.

   J Historical record proves some of the story, but not all.

3. Choose the best paraphrase for this sentence: Mr. Roy gave tours of the house for an admission fee and rented shovels for 50 cents apiece so that visitors could dig for the buried treasure.

   A Mr. Roy collected an admission fee from visitors who wanted to tour the house. He charged an extra 50 cents to rent a shovel. Visitors used the shovels to dig for the buried treasure.

   B Visitors paid money to Mr. Roy because they wanted to tour the house.

   C People visited the house so that they could dig for the buried treasure.

   D Mr. Roy made money from the visitors.

Write the answer to the question.

4. Write a paraphrase of paragraph 18.

   _____

   _____

Explore Words

HARD AND SOFT c AND g

The letter *c* and the letter *g* each have two sounds. In *cavity* and *carrot*, *c* has a hard sound. A hard *c* has the same sound as *k*. A soft *c* has the same sound as the letter *s*, as in *citizen* and *cell*. The letter *g* has a hard sound in words such as *give* and *gorilla*. A soft *g* has the same sound as the letter *j*, as in *cage* and *germ*. Both *c* and *g* usually have a soft sound when they are followed by *e*, *i*, or *y*.

Read each word. Write *hard* or *soft* for the sound of the underlined letter in each word.

1. cash _____

2. action _____

3. garage _____

4. emergency _____

5. giraffe _____

6. curvy _____

SYLLABLES

When a two-syllable word has two consonants in the middle, the syllable division is between them *(con / cept)*. If there is just one consonant in the middle, try dividing it both ways. For example, should *vanish* be *van / ish* or *va / nish*? The first syllable has a short vowel sound, so *van / ish* must be correct.

Draw a line to divide each word into syllables. The first item has been done for you.

1. re / peat

2. outside

3. before

4. console

5. locate

6. spinal

SUFFIXES -y, -en

A suffix is a word part that can be added to the end of words and has meaning. When added to the end of a word a suffix changes the meaning of the word. The suffix *-y* means "characterized by" or "like." The suffix *-en* means "to become" or "made of." *Cloudy* means "characterized by clouds." *Wooden* means "made of wood."

Add the suffix -y or -en to each word to make a word that has the meaning shown.

1. soft_____ means "become soft"

2. rubber_____ means "like rubber"

3. summer_____ means "like summer"

4. straight_____ means "become straight"

5. sharp_____ means "become sharp"

6. mold_____ means "characterized by mold"

MULTIPLE-MEANING WORDS

Some words have more than one meaning. For example, the word *blue* has several meanings. Blue is a color, and it is also a synonym for *sad*. As you read, you may come across multiple-meaning words. You can use context clues to figure out the intended meanings of those words.

Read each sentence. Circle the letter that gives the intended meaning of each underlined word.

1. This year, my daughter's first-<u>period</u> class is algebra.
   a. a type of punctuation
   b. an interval of time
2. The <u>plot</u> of this book is very complicated.
   a. the events in a story
   b. a piece of land
3. Manny will be the <u>pitcher</u> in tomorrow's game.
   a. a position in baseball
   b. a container that holds liquids
4. Fall is my favorite <u>season</u> of the year.
   a. to sprinkle with salt and spices
   b. one of four times of the year

ACADEMIC VOCABULARY

Knowing these high-frequency words will help you in many school subjects.

summary	a brief recap of the main points of something
paraphrase	a restatement of something in one's own words
brief	short
include	to make part of a set
sustain	to cause to continue

Complete the sentences below using one of the words above.

1. Asmera didn't quote the speech exactly, but she wrote a _____ for her brother.

2. Ahmet tried to keep his speech _____ so his audience wouldn't be bored.

3. Ulima sprints really fast, but she can't _____ the speed for long distances.

4. Jorge gave a short _____ of his notes from the meeting.

5. Eun made sure to _____ all the things she would need for her beach trip when she packed.

Lesson 1.5

Identify Cause and Effect

Most stories and many nonfiction passages are built on cause-and-effect relationships. A cause is an action or event that brings about other actions or events, and an effect is the outcome of a cause. Understanding cause-and-effect relationships can deepen your understanding of what you read.

Sometimes a cause-and-effect relationship is directly stated, while other times it is implied. When reading a passage, ask the following questions to determine cause and effect: What happened? Why did it happen?

Writers often use signal words to draw a connection between what happened and why. Here are some words or phrases to look for:

because	since	therefore
so	if/then	as a result

Read these examples:

   Few people visited the sandwich shop, and as a result it went out of business.

What happened? <u>The sandwich shop went out of business.</u> This is the effect.

Why did it happen? <u>Few people visited the sandwich shop.</u> This is the cause.

   Shani felt tired, so she drank a cup of coffee.

What happened? <u>Shani drank a cup of coffee.</u> This is the effect.

Why did it happen? <u>Shani felt tired.</u> This is the cause.

Read the passage. One stated effect is that drakes are unable to fly at the end of the mating season. What is the stated cause?

> Most drakes (male ducks) are brightly colored, so they attract the attention of female ducks during the mating season. However, at the end of the mating season, most drakes molt, or lose their old feathers. Since they no longer have their flight feathers, the drakes are unable to fly. They also lose their bright coloring and turn a drab brown.

The cause is, "They no longer have their flight feathers." The signal word *since* helps show this cause-and-effect relationship.

Read the passage. Then circle the letter of the answer to each question.

A dolphin is not a fish. Like its relatives the whale and the porpoise, a dolphin is a warm-blooded mammal and feeds its young with mother's milk. It breathes the air it needs through a "blowhole" in the top of its head. A dolphin can seal its blowhole with a strong muscle when it is underwater.

Dolphins have torpedo-shaped bodies and smooth, rubbery skin. A strong tail sends the dolphin cruising through the water at speeds up to 18 miles per hour. Dolphins often swim with boats, leaping alongside them or riding the waves created as the boat moves through the water. Dolphins also challenge boats to race by swimming alongside them and then rushing forward to the bow. There they take their place in front of the boat. They may hold this spot for several minutes, as if daring the captain to race.

1. Dolphins are mammals; as a result, they
   A have compound eyes, as bees do.
   B lay eggs, as birds do.
   C have scales, as fish do.
   D nurse their young, as whales do.

2. Dolphins are mammals and breathe through a blowhole; therefore, they
   F must come to the surface of the ocean to breathe.
   G can stay underwater all the time.
   H also have gills.
   J can cover greater distances than whales.

3. Because a dolphin's body is smooth and graceful, the dolphin can
   A breathe air.
   B hide behind rocks.
   C swim fast.
   D feed its young.

4. Since a dolphin's tail is strong, a dolphin is
   F protected from its enemies.
   G a natural hunter.
   H able to break the surface of the water.
   J a powerful swimmer.

Write a cause-and-effect sentence for each passage. Use one of the words or phrases in the box as a signal of the cause-and-effect relationship.

because	since	therefore	as a result	so	if/then

Except for a narrow strip around its shores, Greenland lies buried under a sheet of permanent ice. The ice is thousands of feet thick, and only the tops of the highest mountains extend above it. Icebergs break from these glaciers and drift into the open seas. Sometimes they move thousands of miles to the south before they melt.

1. _____

Although the benefits of aspirin are great, some people cannot take aspirin at all. They get skin rashes or asthma-like reactions even from normal doses. A small number of people who suffer from asthma, hay fever, and other problems may also have a bad reaction to aspirin.

2. _____

_____

Automobile windshields rarely shatter. They may crack, but they do not splinter or fly apart. All vehicles are equipped with windshields made of laminated safety glass. This is like a glass sandwich made of two layers of plate glass with a sheet of plastic in between. This construction helps absorb the energy of an object's impact and keeps the glass from splintering when hit.

3. _____

_____

The fossil remains of clamshells from hundreds of millions of years ago provide clues about the ancient seas of Earth. Fossils are the preserved remains or traces of ancient plants or animals. Scientists examine them closely, like detectives studying fingerprints, to learn the secrets they hold.

4. _____

_____

Read the passage. Then circle the letter of the answer to each question.

Trees are an important natural resource. One man thought they were so important that they deserved a special day of honor. J. Sterling Morton, a journalist and politician, loved trees and was concerned about the speed at which they were disappearing. Many people were cutting down trees without planting new trees in their place. Morton wanted more trees to give shade, stop erosion, and provide building materials. In 1872 he helped convince the Nebraska Board of Agriculture to make April 10 a special day for planting trees. The day was named Arbor Day, because *arbor* is the Latin word for *tree*. The first Arbor Day was a resounding success.

1. What is one intended effect of Arbor Day?

 A More people know about the importance of planting trees.

 B People still cut down trees without planting new ones.

 C Morton stopped being concerned about trees.

 D The holiday lasted only one year.

2. What was one effect Morton expected by planting new trees?

 F He would get a medal for protecting trees.

 G Erosion would increase.

 H People would know that *arbor* means "tree."

 J There would be more trees for building materials.

3. Morton was concerned about disappearing trees, so he

 A tried to stop people from cutting down trees.

 B encouraged people to plant new trees.

 C ran for Congress.

 D stopped using wooden items.

4. The Nebraska Board of Agriculture established Arbor Day because

 F there were too many trees in the state.

 G Morton encouraged them to create the holiday.

 H other states had already celebrated Arbor Day.

 J they were forced to create the holiday by law.

5. Why is the holiday Morton established called Arbor Day?

 A Morton's middle name was Arbor.

 B April is Arbor month.

 C *Arbor* means "tree."

 D An arbor gives shade.

Workplace Skill:
Recognize Cause and Effect in a Performance Assessment Form

You can use cause-and-effect relationships when reading business documents, such as a performance assessment form. Companies use assessment forms to have a regular record of a worker's job performance. The effect of good performance can be a raise or promotion. The causes for firing an employee may be recorded in an assessment form.

Read the assessment form. Then circle the letter of the answer to each question.

Grant Manufacturing Company Performance Assessment Form

Employee Name _____ Job Title _____

Date of Review _____

Performance Assessment Period from _____ to _____

Manager _____

The assessment of your on-the-job performance is based on the ratings assigned to you by your manager. Your performance is compared to the responsibilities and duties stated in your job description. The following rating system is used.

Exemplary	Worker's job performance exceeds expectations and goals every day.
Good	Worker's job performance meets and frequently exceeds expectations and goals.
Average	Worker's job performance is average and occasionally exceeds expectations and goals.
Below Average	Worker's job performance is insufficient and does not meet company expectations.

An employee's performance will be assessed in each of these categories:

Productivity	Teamwork	Creativity	Attitude	Professionalism	Attendance

---

1. Based on the rating scale, what rating would workers get if they usually do only the work expected of them?

   A   Exemplary

   B   Good

   C   Average

   D   Below Average

2. Which result might a worker expect if he or she is continually rated Exemplary in the Productivity, Attitude, and Attendance categories?

   F   At bonus time, the worker will be denied a bonus.

   G   The worker will not get to work on an important, high-priority project.

   H   The worker may be promoted.

   J   After three years, the worker will be reassigned to another division.

Write for Work

Imagine that you are a manager, and it is time for performance assessments of your employees. One of your employees has the following job history:

- He is often late and occasionally gets behind in his assignments.

- He is extremely good at working with other employees on projects.

- He often needs to follow rather than lead in situations but performs his duties adequately.

- He has a good work attitude and occasionally responds to criticism positively.

Use the performance assessment form on page 50 to evaluate this employee. Assign an overall rating. Then write up a performance assessment on this employee in a notebook.

 ## Reading Extension

Turn to "Custer's Last Stand: Battle of Little Bighorn" on page 34 of *Reading Basics Intermediate 2 Reader*. After you have read and/or listened to the article, answer the questions below.

Circle the letter of the answer to each question.

1. What was one effect of the discovery of gold in the Black Hills?
   - **A**   The Sioux wanted to sell the land.
   - **B**   Custer received an award for his discovery.
   - **C**   The government wanted the Sioux to sell their land.
   - **D**   The gold turned out to be fake.

2. What caused President Grant to take away Custer's command?
   - **F**   Grant was angry that Custer testified against Grant's brother.
   - **G**   Grant felt Custer was a proud, overbearing glory hunter.
   - **H**   Grant thought Custer had led poorly during the Civil War.
   - **J**   Grant decided the "boy general" was too young to serve as commander.

3. According to the article, why did Custer lead his men to the Little Bighorn River instead of waiting for Major General Terry?
   - **A**   He wanted the glory of defeating the Plains Indians.
   - **B**   He wanted to impress President Grant.
   - **C**   He wanted to arrive at the meeting point well before schedule.
   - **D**   He didn't want to fight alongside of Major General Terry.

Explore Words

BASE WORDS

A base word is a word that can stand alone and has meaning. You can add prefixes, suffixes, and other endings to a base word, such as *test*.

tests   test**ed**   **pre**test   test**able**

Each word has a prefix, suffix, or other word ending added onto a base word. Circle the prefixes and suffixes. Underline the base words. The first item has been done for you.

1. match(es)
2. misread
3. affordable

4. reformat
5. weakness
6. shorten

SPELLING: POSSESSIVES

Possessive words show that something belongs to a person or thing. The words *Meli's phone* show that the phone belongs to Meli. An apostrophe and *s* (*'s*) is used to write singular possessive words. The words *teachers' coats* show that many coats belong to many teachers. An *s*-apostrophe (*s'*) is used to write plural possessive words.

Read the words. Use apostrophe-*s* (*'s*) or *s*-apostrophe (*s'*) to write possessive words.

1. the classroom that belongs to the students _____

2. the hats that belong to my sisters   _____

3. the CDs that were given to Beto   _____

4. the paints that the artists buy   _____

SYLLABLES

Words consist of one or more syllables. A closed syllable ends in a consonant and has one vowel that is usually short *(hat)*. An open syllable ends with a vowel that is usually long *(go)*. A silent-*e* syllable usually has a long vowel *(late)*.

Unscramble each group of syllables to form a word. Then write the word on the line. The first item has been done for you.

1. tas fan tic   *fantastic*

2. mem re ber _____

3. com re bine _____

4. ket bas ball _____

SILENT CONSONANTS

Some consonant pairs include a silent letter. For example, the *w* is silent in the consonant pair *wr*, as in the word *write*. Some other common consonant pairs are *kn* (silent *k*), *gn* (silent *g*), and *sc* (silent *c*) as in the words *know*, *gnat*, and *scissors*.

Write a word from the box next to its definition. Circle the silent consonant in your answer.

knee	scene	write	wrap	gnome
scent	knock	know	gnat	wrist

1. a portion of a play _____

2. small, imaginary person _____

3. cover something up _____

4. put words on paper _____

5. middle joint of a leg _____

6. a smell _____

7. hit repeatedly _____

ACADEMIC VOCABULARY

Knowing these high-frequency words will help you in many school subjects.

cause   a person or thing that produces an action or condition

effect   a change that is a result or outcome produced by a cause

signal   an event or statement that gives the impulse for something to happen

benefit   the value or advantage gained from something

examine   to inspect or study closely

Complete the sentences below using one of the words above.

1. Aponi did not understand the _____ of her actions until it was too late.

2. He had the _____ of years of experience.

3. The jeweler had to _____ the gems to see if they were real or not.

4. Shakta knew the _____ of the accident: the other driver ran a red light.

5. The umpire gave a _____ that the runner was safe.

Lesson 1.6

Identify Style Techniques

Every writer has his or her own style of writing. Style refers to the way a writer uses words and language to communicate ideas. Some writers have such distinctive styles that a passage of their work could be identified as theirs even without their name on it. A writer's style can be as individual as a fingerprint.

Writing styles can be formal or informal, flowery or concise, dramatic or poetic. An informal style is characterized by short, simple words and sentences. A more formal style uses more difficult words and longer sentences. A flowery style uses very fancy words in long, winding sentences. Some authors use frequent interruptions, creating them by using punctuation such as dashes (—) or colons (:).

In addition to sentence structure and length, writers have other choices that they make that affect their styles. Some writers include many action scenes, while others use dialogue more frequently. Some writers use a lot of description of people and places, while others use description sparingly. These are some of the many ways an author creates a personal style. Remember that writers can use more than one style in a passage. Read the examples:

> Aata meandered through the woods, the crimson and orange leaves crunching under her feet with each step. Small sunbeams shone through the branches, warming her face.

> Aata hiked through the woods. She scaled a rock and snapped a branch off a tree.

The first example uses details to describe how the woods looked and felt. The second example uses shorter sentences to highlight the action.

When you read, take note of the writer's style. Reading different styles of writing can help you learn new ways to express your own ideas.

Read the passage. Then identify which style techniques the writer used.

> Tyrone's heart beat faster as the wagon wheels rolled nearer Brentwood. Before the sun dipped beneath the horizon, he had been able to catch a glimpse of the plantation house with its white pillars and wrought-iron balcony. By some miracle, it was still standing. Four years of civil war had not changed the beautiful old place.

This writer has chosen long sentences and description. The writer uses details to set a scene and paint a picture in words of what the plantation looks like.

Read each writer's description. Then read each passage. Write the label for the writer who most likely wrote the passage. Write an example from the passage that helped you decide.

Writer A uses long, flowing sentences packed with action and adventure.

Writer B uses using short sentences and highly descriptive language that paints effective word pictures.

Writer C uses dialogue extensively to create realistic characters and situations.

Writer D uses punctuation to make frequent interruptions.

"You are always at home or in the office," her friends said to her. "You should go to the theater or the opera."

"Biyen and I have no interest in going to the theater," she answered sedately. "Besides, we have no time for foolishness, and neither of us likes opera."

"Still," her friends would reply, "you need some fun. You work too much."

"Nonsense," she answered. "We both thrive on work."

---

1. _____

_____

Marble—a decorative and durable stone—is prized by some sculptors, builders, and designers. It is a kind of limestone that has been metamorphosed (changed) through the action of heat far below Earth's surface. The heat compresses, or packs down, the limestone. The result—the hard, heavy rock known as marble.

---

2. _____

_____

One sunny day, a fisherman on a large lake struggled with his nets, which were caught on something under the water. He pulled hard, but his nets would not come free. The next day he and a friend returned to the same spot with scuba gear and plunged beneath the waters to investigate. Far beneath the surface, they stared in amazement at the "something" that had fouled the nets. It was an old sailing ship.

---

3. _____

_____

Read each passage and identify one or more style techniques used by the writer. Then write another sentence that continues the passage and uses the style technique(s) found in the passage.

long sentences	descriptive details	dialogue
action	short sentences	interrupting punctuation

> Early one evening during the Depression, Serge stepped off the freight train and stepped into a whirling snowstorm. Serge never even noticed the snow, but he must have felt it seeping down his neck, cold and wet. He must have felt it sopping in his shoes, too, but if you asked him, he wouldn't have known snow was in the air. Even under the bright lights of the main street, Serge didn't see the snowdrifts. He was too hungry, too sleepy, too exhausted.

1. _____

   _____

> I let myself into the dark, quiet apartment and quickly turned on the light so I wouldn't start imagining scary creatures in the shadowy corners. In front of me was Mom's sewing table strewn with purple, red, and green cloth in flowered patterns. Her brown leather sewing box sat on one of the chairs, and a few spools of thread had fallen on the floor. I wondered why my mother had left such a mess when normally she is a very neat person.

2. _____

   _____

> "The computer. For the last time, turn it off and go to bed."
> "You don't understand, Mom. I'm hunting a beast with my guild. If I quit now, everyone's time will be wasted."
> My mother's face gave me my answer. I logged off.
> "There'll be other hunts," she said, not realizing how much effort I had put into this game.

3. _____

   _____

Read each passage. Circle the letter of the style technique used in each passage.

It was a crispy, crackly morning. I hurried across the campus kicking the dried, golden yellow and red leaves. The sun was partially risen, shedding a gold, shimmery color over the plaza. The first puffs of cold autumn air could be felt on the cheeks. It would be a day of memories.

1. A short sentences   **C** interruptions

     B description   **D** dialogue

Frozen desserts date back to the time of Marco Polo, who returned from China with descriptions of fruit ices. Over the years, many different frozen desserts developed, including ice cream, frozen custard, ice milk, and sherbet. The ingredients in these desserts differ, but they have one thing in common: they are best served cold.

2. F dialogue   **H** action

     G long sentences   **J** short sentences

Dogs' noses—which come in all shapes, sizes, and colors—are a mystery. How do they work so well? Scientists don't know everything about how dogs' noses work (although they have certainly tried to find out). A person's sense of smell—by comparison—is very limited. All we can do is marvel (and we do) at the dog's ability to find things with its nose.

3. A dialogue   **C** interruptions

     B short sentences   **D** action

Pop sprang to his feet. "What is it?" he asked. "What has frightened you?"
"It was a wolf, Pop," Minh gulped, catching her breath. "A great big wolf!"
"Where is this wolf now?" Pop shouted.
"I don't know. It ran into the woods," Minh replied.
Minh continued to breathe heavily for several minutes.
"Don't worry, Son," Pop said. "We will be safe here."

4. F description   **H** dialogue

     G long sentences   **J** action

Workplace Skill:
Understand Style Techniques in E-mails

Your writing style is the way you choose words and use them to deliver your message. Most business communications, including memos, e-mails, letters, and policies, are written in a formal style. They have longer, more complex sentences and avoid slang, abbreviations, and contractions. The tone is serious and professional.

Read the following e-mails. Then circle the letter of the answer to each question.

From: Darlene Reed
To: hiring@parkhurstchildcenter.com
Subject: Classroom assistant position

To Whom It May Concern:

I am writing to express my interest in the prekindergarten classroom assistant position you advertised. I have over 10 years of classroom assistant experience in a preschool setting. I also have strong classroom management skills, and I am bilingual in Spanish and English.

I am currently working toward my early-childhood certification. My résumé is attached and further details my experience and certifications, including CPR. Thank you for your time, and I look forward to speaking with you to discuss the position.

Sincerely,
Darlene Reed

From: Darlene Reed
To: KanikaOburumu@abclearning.com
Subject: Job leads

Hey, Kanika. What's up? You've probably heard the news—KidKare Learning had budget cuts and got rid of all the assistants, so I'm pounding the pavement looking for some job leads. Heard of anything? Let me know if anything pops up at your place.

Talk later,
Darlene

---

1. What is the most likely reason the writer wrote the first e-mail in a formal style?

   A because she is writing to a friend

   B because she wants to seem more experienced than she really is

   C because she wants to seem professional

   D because she wants to seem casual

2. Which would be the best way to say "talk later" in a formal style?

   F Talk to you later.

   G Let's catch up another time.

   H I look forward to speaking with you.

   J I have got to go now.

Write for Work

Imagine you see an ad for a position for which you would like to apply. Decide whether you should use a formal or informal writing style, based on your purpose, *why* you are writing, and audience, *whom* you are writing to. Then write an e-mail to the hiring manager expressing your interest and qualifications. Write the e-mail in a notebook.

Workplace Extension

An Interview

1 Savita arrived at the nursing home on time for her interview. She met Judi Rockwell, the woman she had spoken to on the phone. "Thank you for coming so promptly," Judi said to Savita as she showed her into a small office. "Please have a seat and let us talk about why you think you would like to be a food-service worker."

2 "Wow, I'm really glad I got this interview," said Savita. "You don't know how long I've been looking for a job—it seems like forever—if you know what I mean. I've tried it all—even chatting up my friends from school about leads. I love to cook, and I love to eat. Figured I'd be a good match," Savita said, laughing.

Write the answer to each question.

1. What style of language does the speaker use in paragraph 1? Give one example from the paragraph.

_____

_____

2. What style of language does the speaker use in paragraph 2? Give one example from the paragraph.

_____

_____

3. Does Savita respond in the appropriate language for an interview? Why or why not?

_____

_____

Explore Words

r-CONTROLLED VOWELS

When a vowel or vowel pair is followed by the letter *r*, it stands for a different sound. For example, say these word pairs: *chat/chart, flit/flirt, shock/short, heat/hear*. The second word in each pair has an *r*-controlled vowel sound.

Each row includes one word that has an *r*-controlled vowel sound. Say the words aloud. Circle the one that has an *r*-controlled vowel sound. The first item has been done for you.

1. flake	(flare)	flood	friend
2. crazy	crave	curly	clank
3. uptown	upset	upwind	upstairs
4. shirt	shout	sheet	shove

BASE WORDS AND ROOTS

You can add prefixes, suffixes, and other word endings to base words and roots. A base word is a word that can stand alone and has meaning. A root usually cannot stand alone. For example, in *fixable, fix* is a base word, and in *durable, dur* is a root.

Each word includes a base word or root and a suffix or prefix. Underline each base word or root. Circle the suffix or prefix. The first item has been done for you.

1. forget(ful)	**3.** cruelest	**5.** predict
2. sweaty	**4.** mistake	**6.** repeat

SPELLING: CONTRACTIONS

A contraction is a shorter way to write two words. All contractions include an apostrophe ('). The apostrophe takes the place of letters that are dropped to form the contraction. For example, in *I'm*, the apostrophe takes the place of the letter *a* in *I am*.

Match each pair of words on the left with the appropriate contraction on the right.

_____ **1.** should not   **a.** they're

_____ **2.** did not   **b.** hasn't

_____ **3.** we will   **c.** she's

_____ **4.** has not   **d.** didn't

_____ **5.** they are   **e.** we'll

_____ **6.** she is   **f.** shouldn't

SYLLABLES

A syllable is a word or word part that has one vowel sound. When a word includes an *r*-controlled vowel or vowel combination, the vowel or vowel combination and the *r* stay in the same syllable. Many words end in a consonant + -*le*. These letters usually form the final syllable.

Put the syllables together to form a word. Write the word on the line. If the first syllable has an *r*-controlled vowel sound, circle it. If the first syllable has a long vowel sound, underline it. The first one is done for you.

1. mar   ble   ⟨mar⟩ble

2. ti   tle   _____

3. cur   dle   _____

4. cra   dle   _____

5. gir   dle   _____

6. hur   dle   _____

7. cir   cle   _____

8. ma   ple   _____

9. bea   gle   _____

10. spar   kle   _____

ACADEMIC VOCABULARY

Knowing these high-frequency words will help you in many school subjects.

style	a way of using language
individual	characteristic of a particular person or thing
highlight	to pick out and draw attention to
structure	the organization of and relationships between the parts of something
communicate	to share information by speaking, writing, or gesturing

Complete the sentences below using one of the words above.

1. There are many ways to _____ your wishes to your family.

2. Salima had to write an address on each _____ letter.

3. The report's _____ was easy to follow.

4. In his cover letter, Alejando tried to _____ his experience and skills.

5. Zara liked the book's story line, but she didn't care for the author's _____.

Lesson 1.7

Find the Main Idea

Each passage has a topic—what the passage is about—and a main idea—the most important idea. The main idea may be stated in a topic sentence, or the main idea may be implied—not directly stated in the passage. If the main idea is implied, the reader must use the supporting details to determine it.

To find the main idea, read the entire passage and ask yourself what it is about. You may find a sentence that states that idea, but if you do not, the main idea is probably implied. Read the example passage below, in which the main idea is stated:

> Sledding is no longer just a winter sport. In fact, it is even becoming a popular sport in deserts. Desert sledders just head for a sand dune and slide on plastic saucers, pieces of wood, or their own two feet. No matter which kind of sled is used, a great part of the fun is tipping over into the sand.

The topic in the passage above is desert sledding, and the main idea is that desert sledding is becoming popular. It is stated in the second sentence. Often the topic and the main idea will overlap in some way. Read the example below, in which the main idea is implied.

> When humans first gazed at the sky, most concluded that Earth was the center of a system that included the sun, the moon, and many stars. Much later, after telescopes were invented, scientists realized the old model of the universe was incorrect. Today, scientists continue to use telescopes to study space. One telescope is now in orbit around Earth, and an even more powerful telescope is being built to replace it.

The topic of the passage above is telescopes. The implied main idea is that new technologies allow humans to develop more accurate ideas about the universe.

Read the restaurant review. Decide whether the main idea is stated or implied.

> I had heard such good things about Eazy Pizza that I couldn't wait to try it. It took 15 minutes before a hostess greeted us, and when we sat down we had no menus. No one took our drink order or stopped by to greet us. When our pizza arrived almost 45 minutes late, it was barely warm. There were so few pieces of pepperoni that some pizza slices didn't even have any. We all left hungry and disappointed.

The topic of the passage is the writer's experience at Eazy Pizza. The main idea is implied. Although the reviewer never says that he or she does not like Eazy Pizza, all the details work together to imply that Eazy Pizza is not a good pizza place.

Read each passage. Then circle the letter of the answer to each question.

The mudskipper is an unusual fish that can live out of water for several hours. It lives in the tropics in coastal areas along the Atlantic, Pacific, and Indian Oceans, where the falling tides expose large mudflats in river mouths or tidal swamps. Rather than retreating with the tide, mudskippers stay out on the mudflats. They crawl or even hop around on their well-developed front fins. Their eyes stick up on top of their heads. They hunt small crustaceans and other crawling creatures in the mud. As long as the air is not too hot and dry, they can remain out of water until the tide returns, even though they have no lungs.

1. What is the topic of the passage?

   A   the walking fins of a mudskipper

   B   ocean animals

   C   mudflat inhabitants

   D   the mudskipper

2. What is the stated main idea?

   F   The mudskipper is an unusual fish that can live out of water for several hours.

   G   Mudskippers are named for the way they can move around on the mud using their fins.

   H   Some kinds of fish can do things that cannot usually be accomplished by most fish.

   J   Mudskippers hunt creatures in the mud.

Most Americans think that denim is a fabric that originated in the United States. There is a reason for this idea. Back in the late 1800s, in the time of the Old West, Levi Strauss designed sturdy denim pants—blue jeans—to be worn by miners, cowboys, and other people who did hard physical labor. The truth is that the fabric from which jeans are made originated in France, in the city of Nîmes. The French word for *of* is *de*. So when people said that the fabric was "de Nîmes," they meant that it was "of the city of Nîmes," or, more simply, from Nîmes. The French pronunciation for *de Nîmes* sounds similar to *denim*.

3. What is the topic of the passage?

   A   the origin of denim

   B   Levi Strauss and his famous pants

   C   clothes of the Old West

   D   French clothing design

4. What is the implied main idea?

   F   Levi Strauss invented blue jeans in America.

   G   Blue denim fabric was invented in the French city of Nîmes, from which the fabric got its name.

   H   The French contributions to the Old West were important.

   J   The origins of some inventions are surprising.

Read each passage. Then write the implied or stated main idea of each one.

One exotic tree is known to have a thousand or more separate trunks. The banyan tree, which is common in India, has this remarkable structure because of its tough, low-hanging branches. These branches grow down to touch the ground and then develop a set of roots of their own. Each branch becomes a new trunk. If there is enough space and soil, this process goes on until a single tree accumulates a thousand separate trunks, which are all part of the same plant. The largest banyan tree is on the island of Sri Lanka. It has 350 large trunks and more than 3,000 small trunks.

1. _____

_____

The platypus has a bill like a duck's, with hard, flat pads inside it for chewing. The male platypus has sharp spurs on each ankle containing a poison that causes great pain in its enemies. The males use this for defense and for fighting over females during mating season. The platypus has webbed feet like a duck that make it a fine swimmer as well as a tail that helps stabilize it. In fact, it can swim as well as a fish. The females lay small, leathery eggs, and when they hatch, the babies drink their mother's milk. When the platypus gets older, it eats frogs, fish, and freshwater crustaceans. When the first platypus was discovered, nobody could believe that it was real. The platypus is an unusual creature unlike any other mammal.

2. _____

_____

Every year, thousands of giant sea turtles come ashore in Florida and put on a great show for nature lovers. Thousands of people carrying cameras and binoculars line up on Jensen Beach to see the turtles lay their eggs. It's quite a spectacle. Some of these giant sea turtles weigh up to 500 pounds. They lumber ashore, dig nests in the moist sand with their heavy flippers, and deposit their eggs in the holes. Then people watch as the turtles cover the eggs with sand and pay no further attention to them. The warm sun helps the eggs hatch in about two months.

3. _____

_____

Read each passage. Then circle the letter of the answer to each question.

(1) When building their homes, pioneers had to make use of whatever they could find. (2) On the plains, where only a few trees grew, builders faced a serious challenge. (3) So, prairie settlers built their houses with the one thing that was common—sod. (4) The sod, or soil containing grass and roots, was often several inches thick. (5) Packed by rain and hot sun, the sod became so hard that only a sharp plow could cut it. (6) The prairie settlers removed the sod in pieces. (7) The grassy chunks were stacked one on top of the other to form the walls of sod houses.

1. What is the topic of the passage?

  A   the sod houses of the prairie

  B   prairie life

  C   trees that thrive in prairie conditions

  D   growing sod

2. In which sentence is the main idea expressed?

  F   Sentence 1

  G   Sentence 3

  H   Sentence 6

  J   Sentence 7

The North Atlantic Treaty Organization (NATO) was formed to help guard against aggression from the Soviet Union. The Soviet Union collapsed in 1991, and several nations that had once been part of it joined NATO, hoping to remain outside the influence of Russia. By the 21st century, Russia was no longer considered a major threat to NATO nations. Russia and NATO began to cooperate in several areas.

3. What is the topic of the passage?

  A   the North Atlantic

  B   a history of Russia

  C   why several countries were able to resist Russian influence

  D   the relationship between NATO and the Soviet Union

4. Which of the following is the main idea of the paragraph?

  F   NATO and Russia are now allies.

  G   When the Soviet Union collapsed, many countries had to resist Russian influence.

  H   The purpose of NATO has changed over the years.

  J   Russia is still a threat to many nations.

Workplace Skill:
Recognize Main Idea in an Employee Handbook

An employee handbook contains important information about company policies. Most handbooks include such topics as medical insurance, absentee policies, time-off benefits, and dress codes. To understand these kinds of business documents, you need to recognize the main idea and the details that support the main idea.

Read this section from an employee handbook. Then circle the letter of the answer to each question.

Section 5.32: Company-Recognized Holidays

Policy Full-time employees are eligible for 10 paid holidays as follows:

New Year's Day—January 1

Martin Luther King, Jr. Day—Third Monday in January

Presidents' Day—Third Monday in February

Memorial Day—Last Monday in May

Independence Day—July 4

Labor Day—First Monday in September

Thanksgiving Day—Fourth Thursday in November

Day after Thanksgiving Day

Christmas Eve—December 24 (half-day)

Christmas Day—December 25

- If a holiday falls on a Saturday, it will be observed on Friday; if it falls on a Sunday, it will be observed on Monday. If Christmas Eve falls on a Sunday, it will be observed on Friday.

- If an eligible employee works on a holiday, he or she will be paid at the regular straight-time rate for hours worked, in addition to receiving the holiday pay.

---

1. What is the main idea of this section of the employee handbook?

   A to state what happens if a holiday falls on a Saturday

   B to clarify what rate an employee receives if he or she works on a holiday

   C to let employees know when Labor Day occurs during the year

   D to outline the company's holiday pay policy

2. Christmas Eve will fall on a Sunday this year. What day off will be observed by the company?

   F Sunday

   G Saturday

   H Friday

   J Monday

Write for Work

In some companies, employees cannot request a vacation day on a day that comes directly before or after a paid holiday. In a notebook, write a paragraph explaining why a company might adopt this policy. Begin with the main idea, or the main reason that companies would want employees to work on days before or after holidays. Include details and examples that support the main idea.

Workplace Extension

Finishing a Project

Maya Rosini was running behind schedule on the day before the Thanksgiving holiday. She was trying to finish the financial budget she was assigned by her manager. She knew the budget was due early the following week. She had come in early that morning and was getting a good head start on it. She was pleased with herself. Then she realized it was 4 o'clock, and she still wasn't finished. She looked for her boss, but she was in a meeting. Maya decided to stay late to finish the job.

Circle the letter of the answer to each question.

1. What motivated Maya to work late?
   - **A** Her boss told her to stay late.
   - **B** She was trying for a promotion.
   - **C** She wanted to finish her work on schedule.
   - **D** Her boss was working late too.

2. What does Maya's decision demonstrate about her attitude toward her job?
   - **F** It shows she is lazy.
   - **G** It shows she only does what is asked.
   - **H** It shows she is dedicated.
   - **J** It shows she doesn't care.

Write the answer to each question.

3. Imagine you were in Maya's situation on that day. How would you have acted?

_____

4. How do you think the boss reacted when she discovered that Maya had stayed late to finish the job?

_____

_____

Explore Words

VOWEL COMBINATIONS

When two vowels or a vowel + *w* come together, they usually stand for one sound. For example, the letters *ow* stand for the long *o* sound in *glow*. The letters *oo* in *choose* and *ou* in *group* stand for the long *u* sound. Some vowel pairs or a vowel + *w* stand for a different sound. For example, say these words: *noise, boy, house, cow, cause, claw,* and *foot.* In each word, the vowel sound is neither long nor short. It is different.

Say the first word in each row. Circle the other word in the row with the same vowel sound.

1. stood	boot	moose	crook
2. brown	flow	town	crow
3. point	joy	chow	flour
4. June	stool	fault	wood
5. yawn	mouse	pause	praise

SPELLING: WORD ENDINGS -*er*, -*est*

You can add -*er* and -*est* to the end of many adjectives in order to make comparisons. When you add -*er* and -*est*, you may need to change the spelling of the base words.

Add -*er* or -*est* to each word. Write the new word on the line. Change the spelling as necessary. The first one is done for you.

1. happy + -est _____*happiest*_____

2. brave + -er _____

3. fat + -er _____

4. sad + -est _____

5. smart + -er _____

6. lazy + -er _____

SYLLABLES

A syllable is a word part that has one vowel sound. When a vowel or vowel combination is followed by the letter *r*, the vowel(s) and *r* stay in the same syllable. When a word ends with a consonant + *le*, the consonant + *le* form the last syllable.

Divide these two-syllable words into syllables. Then underline the first syllable once if it is short, underline it twice if it is long, and circle it if it is r-*controlled*. The first item has been done for you.

1. turkey _____(tur)/ key_____

2. crater _____

3. sample _____

4. marble _____

When you come across an unfamiliar word in a sentence, you can use context clues to figure out what the unfamiliar word means. You can find context clues in the same sentence or nearby sentences. For example, in this sentence the underlined words are context clues that help you figure out that *pious* means "religious."

My parents are very **pious**, but I am not religious at all.

Use context clues to figure out the meaning of the bold word in each sentence. Write the meaning on the line.

1. The day was **frigid**. Yesterday was not nearly as cold. _____

2. They are **identical** twins, but they don't look exactly the same to me. _____

3. He walked **nonchalantly**, as if he didn't have a care in the world. _____

4. The **summit** of this mountain is higher than the top of that one. _____

5. You should always be polite, even when someone is **discourteous** to you. _____

6. I probably feel **sluggish** because I haven't slept well all week. _____

7. Let's try to **convene** at 2:00, even though a few people will meet earlier. _____

Knowing these high-frequency words will help you in many school subjects.

topic	a subject dealt with in a text or conversation
main	most important
determine	to work out or establish exactly
develop	to bring to a mature state
overlap	to cover part of the same area of interest

Complete the sentences below using one of the words above.

1. The investigators could not _____ the cause of the fire.

2. The _____ of the speech was raising taxes.

3. The _____ road in town is always busy during rush hour.

4. When Julietta was laying tile, she was very careful to line up the pieces so they didn't _____.

5. It is possible to _____ a new allergy at any point in your life.

Unit 1 Review

Recognize and Recall Details

Details give more information about the topic of a passage. Details explain, describe, and clarify. Details can be factual or descriptive.

Understand Stated Concepts

One way to understand and recall what you read is to pay particular attention to the concepts stated in the passage and any words that are defined.

Draw Conclusions

Conclusions are decisions or opinions you form, using facts and your own experiences. Your conclusions are based on things that are stated directly, things that are implied, and things that you already know.

Summarize and Paraphrase

In a summary, you retell the main idea and most important details of a passage. In a paraphrase, you restate the sentences in a passage in your own words. You include most or all of the details.

Identify Cause and Effect

Many passages are built on cause-and-effect relationships. A cause brings about other actions or events. An effect is the outcome of the cause. Sometimes cause-and-effect relationships are directly stated. Other times they are implied.

Identify Style Techniques

Style refers to the way an author uses words and language to express ideas. Word choice, sentence length, the inclusion of details and dialogue, and even the use of punctuation can characterize an author's personal style.

Find the Main Idea

The main idea is the most important idea in a paragraph. It may be stated in a topic sentence or implied. If the main idea is implied, use the supporting details to determine it.

Unit 1 Assessment

Read each passage. Then circle the letter of the answer to each question.

Which comes first, thunder or lightning? You may be surprised to find out that they happen at the same time. We see lightning before we hear thunder because sound and light travel at different speeds. Light travels so fast that you can see lightning almost as soon as it occurs, but sound takes about five seconds to travel a mile. Unless a storm is directly overhead, the sound of thunder will always come after the flash of lightning. The time between the flash of lightning and the sound of thunder signals how close the storm is. If the sound of thunder follows the flash of lightning by 15 seconds, the storm is three miles away.

1. What causes the delay between seeing lightning and hearing thunder?
   - **A** People aren't paying attention during the storm.
   - **B** Sound travels slower than light.
   - **C** Light travels slower than sound.
   - **D** Human ears are slower than human eyes.

2. If you hear thunder 15 seconds after you see lightning, your distance from the storm is
   - **F** one mile.
   - **G** two miles.
   - **H** three miles.
   - **J** not known.

You may know how to identify some trees by their leaves, but did you know that a tree can also be identified by its bark? The barks of various trees differ in thickness and color. Some trees, such as the birch, have smooth, papery bark that peels off in layers. Other trees, such as redwood and oak, have one rough, thick layer of bark. It cracks and breaks as the tree trunk grows larger. The colors of bark range from the white of some birch trees to the dark brown of the walnut tree. Whatever its thickness or color, bark protects a tree against bad weather, insects, and even forest fires.

3. What is the best summary of this passage?
   - **A** Trees have different kinds of bark. Some bark is smooth. Some bark is rough. Bark is different colors.
   - **B** You can identify a tree more easily by looking at its bark than at its leaves. Some bark looks like paper and peels off one layer at a time. Some bark breaks off as the trunk gets larger. Bark protects trees.
   - **C** Some trees have smooth bark that comes off in layers, such as a birch tree. Oak trees have rough dark brown bark. Bark protects the trees from damage.
   - **D** Trees can be identified by both their leaves and their bark. Different kinds of trees have different kinds of bark. The bark is different in thickness and color depending on the type of tree. Bark protects trees.

The question "Do bananas grow on trees?" is a slippery one. The plant's large, droopy green leaves certainly make it look like a tree. Its stalk even grows to a height of 8 to 30 feet. However, the tall banana stalk contains no woody fibers and is therefore not classified as a tree. Only one bunch of bananas grows on a stalk at any one time. A freshly cut bunch of green bananas may weigh as much as 100 pounds.

4. What is the main idea of this passage?

F Bunches of bananas are larger than people think.

G The banana tree contains no woody fibers but can grow to heights of 8 to 30 feet.

H Despite its height and appearance, the plant that bananas grow on is not considered a tree.

J Even though it is not really a tree, the banana plant can produce a lot of fruit at one time.

5. How much can a freshly cut bunch of bananas weigh?

A 8 pounds

B 10 pounds

C 30 pounds

D 100 pounds

Bottles and glasses are like soap bubbles that endure instead of popping and fading away. A glassmaker heats the ingredients that make glass—silica sand, limestone, and soda ash—until they become a melted, syrupy mixture. A ball of that mixture is attached to the end of an iron glass-blowing pipe. The blower then puffs air gently into the other end of the pipe. The glass inflates in much the same way as a soap bubble does. Expert glassblowers can mold the bubble into any shape they want it to be. As long as the glass is being heated, it can be shaped and reshaped. When the glassblower is satisfied with the glass creation, it is set aside to cool and harden.

6. What is a good paraphrase of the last two sentences from the passage?

F Glass can be molded as long as it is hot.

G The glassblower should keep the glass hot until he or she is satisfied with the shape.

H Glassblowers keep glass hot until they are satisfied with the shape they have created. It is difficult for them to maintain the right temperature while they work.

J Glass can be molded and shaped as long as it is hot. Once it cools, it hardens and keeps its shape.

7. What is one tool a glassblower uses?

A a soap bubble

B an iron pipe

C a bottle

D a copper pipe

8. What causes the glass to inflate?

F air puffed into a pipe

G a change in temperature

H the addition of soda ash

J the cooling process

Before dawn, Kye was awakened by a crashing sound. He leapt to his feet in the dim light and saw the back of a huge, fur-covered creature. It was rummaging through his food. Kye reached for his gun and waited to see what the creature would do next. It growled and then turned to face Kye, looking more like a gigantic man than an animal. It stood upright like a man, but it must have weighed at least 1,000 pounds. After staring at Kye for what seemed like forever, the creature snatched some food in its front, hand-like paws and then disappeared into the brush with a few long strides.

9. Identify the style techniques that the author is using.

   A   action and description

   B   short sentences and interruption

   C   dialogue and action

   D   description and interruption

10. Based on the facts in the passage and your own experience, what do you think Kye saw?

   F   a dog

   G   a bear

   H   a raccoon

   J   a man

In the past, famine or disease killed people at an early age. The death rate among young people was high, and the birth rate was low. With modern advances in health care, agriculture, and sanitation, life spans have increased, resulting in an enormous increase in population.

11. One cause of the increase in population is

   A   low birth rate.

   B   famine.

   C   advances in health care.

   D   high death rate among young people.

12. What is one thing that lead to death at a young age in the past?

   F   medical care

   G   advances in agriculture

   H   famine

   J   low birth rate

13. What is the main idea of this passage?

   A   Modern advances have led to an increase in population.

   B   People died from many different causes in the past.

   C   Modern people have it better than people in the past.

   D   These days, people live much longer than they did in the past.

14. What style technique does the writer use?

   F   dialogue

   G   action

   H   descriptive details

   J   long sentences

Read the memo. Then circle the letter of the answer to each question.

> **From:** Human Resources
>
> **To:** All Employees
>
> **Subject:** Company Holiday Party
>
> (1) Special activities are being planned to make this year's holiday party fun and festive, and we hope that many of you will participate. (2) No one will be pressured to take part. (3) But be careful that you don't miss out on some of the fun! (4) There are many ways for you to get involved.
>
> (5) The first scheduled event is a costume parade and contest, which will be judged by our president. (6) The best-kept secret is that everyone will get a prize. (7) The production group is also organizing some games and asking for volunteers to be contestants. (8) Finally, the writers in our company are creating skits and looking for people who like to sing and act. (9) No talent is necessary, but a good sense of humor is a must.
>
> (10) We hope that all of you will be able to attend what promises to be our best holiday party ever.

15. The main idea of the first paragraph is stated in

   A sentence 1.

   B sentence 2.

   C sentence 3.

   D sentence 4.

16. If people do not participate in the special activities,

   F they will be required to sing at next year's party.

   G the president of the company will be displeased.

   H they will get prizes anyway.

   J they will miss out on some of the fun.

17. What will happen if you lose the costume contest?

   A Your coworkers will be disappointed.

   B You won't get a prize.

   C You will have to clean up after the party.

   D You will get a prize anyway.

18. Which of these is the best paraphrase of sentence 5 in the memo?

   F Our president will take part in the costume parade and contest.

   G You can watch a costume parade and contest.

   H A costume parade will begin the evening.

   J Our president will judge the costume parade and contest.

19. If someone wants to participate in skits, what must he or she have?

   A a costume

   B a good singing voice

   C a sense of humor

   D skill at game playing

20. What prizes will be awarded?

   F extra time off

   G chocolates

   H a picture in the company newsletter

   J not stated

Read the procedure document. Then circle the letter of the answer to each question.

Procedure for Preparing Files for Storage

- All files that have not been active for three or more years should be sent to the company archive. To determine if a file is active, you must review the modification date of the file. Do not rely on the date in the file name or the date used in the header or footer.

- Rename the file using the storage file naming convention. The file name should include the project code, the component abbreviation, the project supervisor's initials, and the abbreviation INAC. See the example code below:

  H9572_PF_AH_INAC

  H9572 = Project Code
  PF = Component Abbreviation
  AH = Supervisor's Initials
  INAC = Inactive

- For a full list of project codes, supervisors, and component abbreviations, please check the company's wiki.

- When file naming is complete, place all inactive files on the storage server in the appropriate project folder.

- Contact the archiving department to let them know there are files on the server to be archived.

21. What should be included in the name of the file?

A the project code, the component abbreviation, the supervisor's initials, the abbreviation INAC, and the date

B the project code, the supervisor's initials, the component abbreviation, and the abbreviation INAC

C the project code, the supervisor's initials, and the component abbreviation

D the project code, the component abbreviation, the supervisor's initials, and the date

22. How should you decide if a file needs to be archived?

F Look at the date used in the footer.

G Look at the date used in the file name.

H Look at the date used in the header.

J Look at the date the file was last modified.

23. What should you do once you have named the file?

A Check the modification date.

B Contact the archiving department.

C Place the file on the company's wiki.

D Place the file on the storage server in the appropriate project folder.

24. What is a reasonable conclusion to draw from this document?

F The company wants its archived files to be organized.

G The company does not care about file storage.

H The company hopes to print its archives.

J The company assumes the people who work there can create their own storage methods.

Circle the letter of the answer to each question.

25. Which consonant blend completes the word in the following sentence?

Edita made a box out of _____ap wood.

A nt

B thr

C sk

D scr

26. What is the plural form of *wolf*?

F wolves

G wolfs

H wolfes

J wolffs

27. What is the correct contraction for *you are*?

A youre

B you're

C your

D your'e

28. Which consonant pair completes the word in the following sentence?

Issa resi_____ed from her job.

F wr

G sc

H gn

J kn

29. What is the correct way to rewrite the sentence below?

The notebooks of the students were full.

A The students's notebooks were full.

B The student's notebooks were full.

C The students' notebooks were full.

D The students notebooks were full.

30. Which word has an *r*-controlled vowel?

F stairs

G chain

H stay

J stripe

31. Which word fits into both sentences?

Cleto paid the _____ on time.

The duck carried a worm in its _____.

A tab

B beak

C check

D bill

32. Which word means "the most pretty"?

F prettyer

G prettyest

H prettier

J prettiest

Choose the word that means the same or about the same as the underlined word. For the second question, use context clues to help you. Circle the letter of the answer to each question.

33. clever student

A foolish

B smart

C top

D enthusiastic

34. Piao felt queasy right after eating lunch. Could the food have been spoiled?

F hungry

G sick

H sad

J angry

Unit 2

In this unit you will learn how to

You will practice the following workplace skills

You will also learn new words and their meanings and put your reading skills to work in written activities. You will get additional reading practice in *Reading Basics Intermediate 2 Reader*.

Lesson 2.1

Identify Sequence

When you read, it is important to determine the order in which things happen. This time order, or sequence, will help you understand how events, concepts, and themes relate to one another. Information is often, but not always, presented in the order in which events happened. Writers may relate events out of order to build suspense, emphasize connections, or highlight important occurrences. Look for words that signal time order such as *first, before, next, after, last,* and *then*. These clue words can help you to identify the sequence. Read the example and notice the sequence of events:

> For 10 months, the United States and Great Britain airlifted supplies into West Berlin. This happened during the Cold War when the Soviet Union blockaded ground supply routes. Lieutenant Gail S. Halvorsen noticed children watching the planes come in. After talking with a group of these children, he began to drop from his plane tiny parachutes with candy and gum attached. Other pilots and crews soon began dropping the parachutes and became known as the "Candy Bombers."

In the passage above, the writer uses clue words to tell you the order of events. Words such as *during, when, after,* and *soon* are signal words to help you understand sequence. Notice that the events concerning Lieutenant Halvorsen happened during the time period described in the first and second sentences, not after it.

Read the passage. In a notebook, put the events in order of what happened first, next, and last.

> Many of the earliest peoples to live in North America came from Siberia, crossing a land bridge that is now covered by the Bering Sea. At first, they hunted big game animals such as mastodons and large bison, but over time, these animals died out. While some groups began to hunt smaller animals, others lived by gathering roots, plants, and berries. These people are known as hunter-gatherers. Even later, some people learned how to grow crops from the plants and seeds they gathered. These people became farmers.

In the passage above, key phrases such as *at first, over time,* and *even later* indicate the sequence in which the events described occur. First, people were big game hunters. Next, they became hunter-gatherers. Finally, they learned to farm.

Sometimes you will read instructions that explain how to do something. The sequence of steps in the instructions will be very important, especially if the steps are not numbered. Clue words such as *first*, *then*, *before*, *after*, *next*, and *finally* will help you complete the steps in the correct order.

Read the passage. Then follow the directions.

How many times have you taken pictures of your friends and family and wished you could be in the picture, too? Once you learn how to use the self-timer button on your digital camera, you can always be a part of a group picture. First, organize the people you want to take a picture of into a group, making sure to leave a space for yourself. Next, turn on the self-timer button on your camera. Set your camera on a flat, even surface that has plenty of room. Now, push the shutter button halfway to focus the camera and check your screen to make sure the picture is the way you want it. Then, push the button the rest of the way and move into your spot. As you push the button, make sure you don't move the camera from its position.

Write the steps in order.

1. _____

2. _____

3. _____

4. _____

5. _____

6. _____

7. _____

8. _____

Write words from the passage that helped you understand the order of events.

9. _____

_____

_____

Read the passage. Then follow the directions below.

> One day in July 1938, Douglas Corrigan raced his light plane down the runway of an airfield in New York. Before the flight, authorities had rejected Corrigan's plan to fly across the Atlantic, but they gave him permission to fly from California to New York and back. When Corrigan took off down the runway, everyone at the airport was surprised to see him headed toward the Atlantic Ocean instead of California. A day later, the airplane mechanic and pilot touched down in Ireland. Afterward, the authorities asked Corrigan why he landed in Ireland instead of California. He answered, "My compass must have been wrong. I must have flown in the wrong direction. I thought I was over California, but when I came down to see where I was, there was nothing but water." The flight made Corrigan famous, and from then on he was known as "Wrong Way."

Put the sentences in order to show the sequence of events.

1. _____   **a.** Authorities gave permission for Corrigan to fly from California to New York and back.

2. _____   **b.** Corrigan took off from New York.

3. _____   **c.** People began calling Corrigan "Wrong Way."

4. _____   **d.** Corrigan told authorities he had flown the wrong way.

5. _____   **e.** People were surprised to see Corrigan fly toward the Atlantic Ocean instead of California.

6. _____   **f.** Corrigan asked permission to fly across the Atlantic.

7. _____   **g.** Corrigan landed in Ireland.

8. _____   **h.** Authorities denied Corrigan permission to fly across the Atlantic.

Write words and dates from the passage that helped you understand the order of events.

9. _____

_____

_____

_____

_____

Read the passage. Then circle the letter of the answer to each question.

Betty Friedan was an author and a leader of the women's rights movement. After she graduated from Smith College in 1942, she became a freelance writer and political activist. Her most famous book, *The Feminine Mystique*, was published in 1963. The book grew from surveys that she had taken of her Smith College classmates in 1957, years after they graduated. These surveys showed that despite their education and subsequent successes, they were unhappy with their lives. The book became a best seller. In 1966 Friedan and other feminists formed the National Organization for Women (NOW). NOW works to get women access to education and employment equal to that of men, among other issues.

1. What did Friedan do in 1942?

   A She published *The Feminine Mystique*.

   B She founded NOW.

   C She graduated from Smith College.

   D She circulated a survey among her classmates.

2. How many years elapsed between the release of *The Feminine Mystique* and the founding of NOW?

   F 3

   G 9

   H 11

   J 24

3. When did Friedan survey her Smith College classmates?

   A before she entered the college

   B while she was a student at Smith College

   C more than a decade after she graduated

   D after she founded NOW

4. According to the passage, what did Friedan do right after she graduated from Smith College?

   F She founded NOW.

   G She circulated a survey among her classmates.

   H She became a freelance writer and political activist.

   J She published *The Feminine Mystique*.

5. In what year did Friedan help to form the National Organization for Women?

   A 1942

   B 1957

   C 1963

   D 1966

Workplace Skill:
Use Sequence to Write a Résumé

Whether you are applying for your first job or trying to get a better job, a good résumé can help you stand out from the crowd. A résumé is a list of all your qualifications, or skills, and past work experience. Your résumé is your first chance to make a good impression on an employer. If possible, use a computer when you write your résumé.

Read the instructions. Then circle the letter of the answer to each question below the box.

How to Write a Résumé

First, type your name, address, phone number, and e-mail address. Make sure you type this information correctly because it is how a potential employer will be able to contact you.

Next, type a strong and focused objective statement. An objective statement is a sentence or two that focuses on what kind of job you want. Be sure that this statement corresponds to the job for which you are applying. For example, if you are applying to be a waitress, you might write: *I want a service career in the restaurant industry.* Write your objective statement carefully. It is one of the first things an employer will see.

Now you are ready to list your education history and work experience. First, name the schools you have attended, their location, and the year of any degrees or certificates you received.

Next, list your work history. Start with your most recent job and state your position, title, and the dates you held this job. Then list what you achieved, or accomplished, in this position. If you are applying for your first job, list internships, volunteer experience, or school activities.

List any relevant skills. This would include computer programs you know and any special training you may have, such as CPR or lifeguard certification.

Finally, include references. References are people that your future employer can call or contact to learn more about you. References can be people you have worked for, teachers, or people who have known you for a long time. Choose people who can explain why you would be a good employee. Do not list relatives.

Before you send your résumé, review it carefully and check that it is neat, organized, and has no mistakes. Use spell-check. Aim to catch all the grammatical and punctuation errors and all typographical mistakes as well. Also ask someone to double-check that everything is correct.

1. What should you list on a résumé after you have listed your education?

   A your objective statement

   B your references

   C your contact information

   D your work history

2. Why is it important to write a strong and focused objective on a résumé?

   F It lists your skills and accomplishments.

   G It shows that you want the type of job for which you are applying.

   H It helps describe the kind of person you are.

   J It shows that you are applying for your first job.

Write for Work

You are applying for a new job. In a notebook, write your own résumé. Use the instructions for writing a résumé on page 82. Follow the sequence of steps as listed.

 **Reading Extension**

Turn to "Kim's Story: The Big Bubble" on page 42 of *Reading Basics Intermediate 2 Reader*. After you have read and/or listened to the article, answer the questions below.

Circle the letter of the answer to each question.

1. What event happened at the same time Kimberly saw the bubble?
   - **A** Kimberly drew a picture of the ship.
   - **B** Mrs. Baker believed that Kimberly had seen a UFO.
   - **C** Kimberly discovered the pussy willow stems were too tough to break.
   - **D** A neighbor's dog barked loudly.

2. How many days passed between the time Kimberly saw the UFO and the time she spoke with Allie King?
   - **F** two days
   - **G** four days
   - **H** 11 days
   - **J** 15 days

3. What event happened after Kimberly spoke to Allie King?
   - **A** Kimberly saw a man with lots of black buttons on his chest.
   - **B** Kimberly drew a picture of the ship.
   - **C** Kimberly took her mother and King to the place where she'd seen the ship.
   - **D** King tried to confuse Kimberly.

Write the answer to each question.

4. What is the earliest event described in the article?

   _____

   _____

5. What event happened after Kimberly told her mother about the bubble?

   _____

   _____

Explore Words

A prefix is a word part that can be added to the beginning of many words. Adding a prefix changes the meaning of the word to which it is added. For example, the prefix *mis-* means "wrong" or "badly," so the word *misbehaves* means "behaves badly." The prefix *un-* means "not" or "the opposite of," so *unwelcoming* means "not welcoming."

Read each sentence. Choose *mis-* or *un-* to complete the word. Write the prefix on the line.

1. The boss was _____impressed with my report.

2. It is common to _____pronounce that word.

3. You must have _____understood the task.

4. His visit was totally _____expected, but I was so happy to see him.

5. I will try to get rid of my _____healthy habits.

6. My unusual name is often _____spelled.

7. Silvio thought the mistake was _____important.

8. Aida _____intentionally left her off the guest list.

SYNONYMS

Synonyms are words that have the same or almost the same meaning. For example, *answer* and *reply* are synonyms.

Choose a synonym from the box for each word in parentheses. Write the word on the line.

announce	commence	distress	plausible
avoid	disappeared	gratitude	vacant

1. The loss of his dog has caused him much _____. (anguish)

2. You can't _____ this problem forever. (ignore)

3. In the mystery, the girl _____ without a trace. (vanished)

4. Do you have a _____ explanation for being so late? (believable)

5. The news report will _____ the winner of the election. (disclose)

6. My aunt expressed her _____ for all our help. (appreciation)

7. The event will _____ early in the morning. (begin)

8. The building has been _____ for nearly a year. (empty)

You can add the endings *-ed* and *-ing* to most verbs to change the form. When you add *-ed* or *-ing*, remember these spelling rules:

- When a word ends with silent *e*, drop the *e*. Then add *-ed* or *-ing*.

  manage   manag<u>ed</u>   manag<u>ing</u>

- When a two-syllable word ends with one vowel and one consonant, double the last consonant if the accent is on the second syllable. Then add *-ed* or *-ing*. If the accent is on the first syllable, just add *-ed* or *-ing*.

  re ´**pel**   repe<u>lled</u>   repe<u>lling</u>

  ´**rea** son   reason<u>ed</u>   reason<u>ing</u>

Add the ending to each word. Write the new word on the line.

1. admit + ed   _____

2. prepare+ed   _____

3. refuse + ing   _____

4. focus + ed   _____

5. dispute + ing   _____

6. label + ed   _____

7. season +ed   _____

8 upset+ ing   _____

Knowing these high-frequency words will help you in many school subjects.

sequence	the order in which things are connected
concept	an idea
theme	an idea that reoccurs in or continues through a work of art or literature
survey	an investigation into the opinions or experience of a group of people by asking them questions
subsequent	following

Complete the sentences below using one of the words above.

1. Her divorce and _____ remarriage all happened quickly.

2. One _____ that comes through in all of Johnson's books is loneliness.

3. Chaytan had a good _____, but his design didn't work out in the execution.

4. If Ozoro had followed the steps in the correct _____, her table wouldn't be missing a leg.

5. Fill out this _____ to share your reactions to the current health insurance plan.

Lesson 2.2

Understand Consumer Materials

INTRODUCE

A consumer is someone who buys things for his or her own use. All people are consumers, whether they buy a lot or a little. People buy, or consume, products as well as services. For example, they might buy a product such as a washing machine and a service plan to extend the warranty. Service providers include dentists, plumbers, and home-health aides.

Materials that are associated with the things people buy are called consumer materials. There are many different kinds of consumer materials, including advertisements, coupons, product labels, instructions, owner's manuals, and forms related to services. It is important to read consumer materials carefully. They may contain critical information that you need know in order to use or maintain your product or to access certain services.

Coupons are one type of consumer material. You may use coupons when you purchase things that you need or want. Coupons can work in a variety of ways, including giving a percent discount, a specific dollar amount discount, or a free item. Some coupons have different values depending on the amount of your purchase, while others restrict the items that can be purchased with the coupon.

Expires 9/27

COMPLIMENTARY

Coffee **Café**

small size prepared drink with drink purchase of same size or larger.

Limit one per customer. Cannot be combined with any other promotions or coupons. Good while supplies last. Void where prohibited. Valid for coffee drinks only. Maximum value of free item $4.75.

(12)345678(90)12

Most coupons contain the following items: name of the store or product associated with the coupon, an expiration date, the offer, the restrictions, and a bar code. Look at the example coupon.

The coupon above gives the expiration date of the coupon in the upper right corner. The offer takes up most of the coupon, and the restrictions are below it in very small print. Not every coupon will have a bar code, but most include them for the cashier to scan as you make your purchase.

Look at the coupon above and answer the questions below.

> What must you do to receive a free drink? Can you use this coupon with a 20% off coupon to the same café? If you want an herbal tea, can you get it with this coupon?

To receive a free drink, you must buy another drink in the small size or a larger size. You cannot use this coupon with your 20% off coupon. The restrictions tell you that you cannot combine this coupon with other coupons. You cannot request an herbal tea with this coupon because it is valid for coffee drinks only.

Many products come with manuals that give directions for their care and maintenance. You should read the manual to familiarize yourself with the requirements of your product.

Read this excerpt from a car owner's manual. Then answer the questions.

When to Add Engine Oil

You should add at least one quart of oil if the oil is below or at the ADD line on the dipstick. Be careful not to add too much oil. If the oil level goes above the MAX line of your dipstick, your engine could be damaged.

What Kind of Oil to Use

SAE 10W-30 is the best oil to use in this vehicle. You can use SAE 5W-30 if you regularly drive in temperatures lower than 60°F. Do not use other viscosities, or thicknesses, of oil because these can severely damage your engine. You can tell the viscosity of the oil you are buying by the numbers on the oil container. For your convenience, the recommended oil viscosity for your vehicle is also printed on the oil cap in your engine.

6-12

1. When should you add more oil to your engine?

_____

_____

2. What is the recommended oil for normal driving?

_____

_____

3. What could happen if you add too much oil?

_____

_____

4. How can you tell the viscosity of the oil you are buying?

_____

_____

5. Where besides the owner's manual can you find out what kind of oil to use?

_____

_____

Occasionally, products do not work in the way the manufacturer intended. When that happens, the manufacturer will often issue a recall. If you discover that a product you have purchased is subject to a recall, it is important to read the recall notice carefully to find out what to do.

Read the product recall and answer the questions.

FOR IMMEDIATE RELEASE   **Brierley Appliance (888) 555-1234**
June 18

In compliance with the U.S. Consumer Products Safety Commission (CPSC), Brierley Appliance Company of San Diego, California, is voluntarily recalling 3,200 toasters. The lever on the toaster can become stuck and cause the heating element to stay on indefinitely. This can cause a fire hazard.

Brierley Appliance has received 25 reports of the toaster overheating. There has been one report of fire, resulting in $1,340 worth of damage. The recalled toasters have a black lever, and the case is either white or red. They were sold at home and appliance stores between January and March for about $18.

Consumers should stop using these toasters immediately and contact Brierley Appliance at (888) 555-1234 to request a free replacement toaster. For more information, call (888) 555-1234 or visit the Brierley Appliance website, www.brierleyappliance.com.

1. If you have a Brierley toaster that you purchased in December that has a blue case, what should you do? Why?

_____

_____

2. If you have a red Brierley toaster that you purchased in February that has not overheated, what should you do? Why?

_____

_____

3. How much will you have to pay for a replacement if your toaster is part of the recall?

_____

_____

4. If you are unsure whether your toaster is part of the recall, what should you do?

_____

_____

Read the excerpt from the drug facts label for cough syrup. Then circle the letter of the answer to each question.

Ask a doctor before use if you have • liver disease • cough that occurs with too much phlegm • glaucoma • a sodium-restricted diet	
When to use this product • do not use more than directed • excitability may occur • drowsiness may occur • do not drink alcohol • be careful operating heavy machinery or driving	
Directions • take only as directed • use dose cup or tablespoon (TBSP) • do not exceed 4 doses in 24 hours	
Adults and children 12 years and over	2 TBSP every 6 hrs
Children 4 to 12 years	Ask a doctor
Children under 4 years	Do not use

1. What does TBSP stand for?

  A teaspoon

  B tablet

  C tablespoon

  D times

2. Who should ask a doctor before using this medicine?

  F everyone

  G children under four years old

  H adults who are on a sodium-restricted diet

  J adults who are not on a sodium-restricted diet

3. What feelings might you experience as a result of using this product?

  A drowsiness or anger

  B sadness or excitability

  C drowsiness or excitability

  D anger or sadness

4. How much cough medicine should you take per dose?

  F 1 tablespoon

  G 2 tablespoons

  H 4 tablespoons

  J 6 tablespoons

5. How much medicine can you take each day?

  A 1 dose

  B 4 doses

  C 6 doses

  D 24 doses

6. What should you do if you have glaucoma?

  F Ask a doctor before taking the medicine.

  G Expect to develop a cough.

  H Take 2 tablespoons.

  J Follow a sodium-restricted diet.

Workplace Skill:
Use Consumer Materials: Waiver of Group Health Coverage Form

Consumer materials are documents that are written for the consumers, or purchasers, of goods or services. Many employees participate as consumers in their company's health-care plans. Employees can elect to participate in these plans and typically contribute a certain dollar amount from their paychecks each month to the cost.

Read the form. Then circle the letter of the answer to each question below the box.

Waiver of Group Health Coverage

Company Name: _____

Employee's Name: _____ Date of Birth: _____

Please Check One:

☐   I waive my employer's group health insurance coverage for myself and my dependents (if any).

☐   I am enrolling in my employer's group health insurance coverage, but I am waiving coverage for my dependents.

Reason for Waiving Coverage—Please Check One:

☐   Covered through spouse's employer:

Employer Name: _____

Insurance Company: _____

☐   Other reason (explain): _____

_____

As a result, I waive my and/or my dependents' (if any) eligibility to enroll in my employer's group plan at this time. I understand that I and/or my dependents may enroll under this plan in the future only within 30 days of involuntary loss of other group coverage or at the time of my employer's annual open enrollment.

Employee Signature: _____ Date: _____

---

1. Employees are required to sign the form. Why should this be a requirement?

   A to ensure that the employees read and agreed to the waiver

   B to accept enrollment in the employer's health-care plan

   C to apply within 30 days of involuntary loss of coverage

   D to elect to enroll a dependent in the heath-care plan

2. What does the word *waive* mean as used in the form?

   F to make a physical movement of the arm

   G to be in doubt about something

   H to voluntarily give up a privilege or claim

   J to seek enforcement of a claim

Write for Work

Think about a consumer document that you are familiar with, such as a food label or a newspaper advertisement. Write the purpose of the document in a notebook. Include the kind of information you usually find in the document.

 **Reading Extension**

Turn to "Poison on the Drugstore Shelf" on page 50 of *Reading Basics Intermediate 2 Reader*. After you have read and/or listened to the article, answer the questions below.

Circle the letter of the answer to each question.

1. If the victims had read the drug use information, would it have helped them?
    A   Yes; they would have taken the correct dosage.
    B   Yes; they would have known they were taking poison and refrained from swallowing it.
    C   No; they would not have understood the instructions and still would have taken the pills.
    D   No; the instructions would not mention cyanide because it was not supposed to be in the bottle.

2. What was one effect of the Tylenol tragedy?
    F   Packages now have multiple safety seals.
    G   Pills are often packaged in individual plastic packs.
    H   People cannot add poison to capsules.
    J   The Tylenol killer was caught and imprisoned.

3. Why were people afraid to buy anything at grocery stores?
    A   They were afraid of eating bad chocolate.
    B   They were afraid that the killer had poisoned more items.
    C   They were afraid that Tylenol had gotten into the items.
    D   They were afraid that they wouldn't be able to get past the safety seals.

Write the answer to each question.

4. How did cyanide get into the Tylenol bottles?

   _____

   _____

5. What could have helped to prevent the contamination of Tylenol bottles?

   _____

Explore Words

A contraction is a short way to write two words. The contraction *isn't* is a shorter way to write the words *is not*. The apostrophe (') in *isn't* takes the place of the letter *o* in *not*.

On the lines below, write the contraction for each pair of words.

1. do not _____

2. we are _____

3. should not _____

4. would not _____

5. are not _____

6. he is _____

SUFFIXES *-ive, -ish*

A suffix is a word part that can be added to the end of a word. Adding a suffix to a word changes its meaning. For example, the suffix *-ive* means "tending to," so *active* means "tending to act." The suffix *-ish* means "like," so *childish* means "like a child."

Complete each sentence, adding the suffix *-ive* or *-ish* to each word in parentheses. Write the word on the line.

1. The coat was _____ in color. (yellow)

2. The man is 80, but he still has a _____ smile. (boy)

3. He is being very _____ about his salary. (secret)

4. We are the baby's _____ parents. (adopt)

BASE WORDS AND ROOTS

Many words in English consist of base words or roots to which prefixes, suffixes, and other endings have been added. Base words and roots contain the main meaning of a word. A base word can stand alone, while a root cannot. For example, in the word *repayment*, *pay* is a base word. In the word *invisible*, *vis* is a root.

Read each group of words. Underline any prefixes, suffixes, or other endings. Then circle the two words in each row that have the same base word or root.

1. previewed   reverted   interviewing

2. disruptive   interrupt   distracted

3. transport   portable   depart

As you read, you may come across words you do not know. You can use context clues to figure out what these unfamiliar words mean. Context clues are words in the same sentence or in nearby sentences that help you understand the meaning of the unfamiliar word.

Write the meaning of each underlined word on the line.

1. In tests, go with your <u>initial</u> answer. Your first idea is often correct.

   Initial means _____.

2. Years ago, people kept food cold with blocks of ice. Today, we no longer have to use this old, <u>outmoded</u> method.

   Outmoded means _____.

3. The summer temperatures in our area <u>fluctuate</u>. Some days are cool, and some days are hot.

   Fluctuate means _____.

4. This year we learned about <u>taxonomy</u>, the groupings of plants and animals.

   Taxonomy means _____.

ACADEMIC VOCABULARY

Knowing these high-frequency words will help you in many school subjects.

consume   to eat, drink, buy, or use up

instructions   directions or orders

excerpt   a short extract from a longer piece of writing

request   to ask for

specific   clearly defined or identified

Complete the sentences below using one of the words above.

1. Hui-ying had to _____ the days she wanted to take off for her vacation.

2. Nkeka needed a _____ type of fabric to create the right look for the dress she was making.

3. Jorgé read an _____ from the book before he decided to read the whole thing.

4. The _____ that came with my DVD player were hard to follow.

5. Modern people _____ many more goods than people did in the past.

Lesson 2.3

Use Reference Sources

You may need to do research at different times. You may want information about a famous person or a country you want to visit. You may need to research a topic for work or school. There are many different reference sources that can help you locate information.

Encyclopedias, dictionaries, and almanacs are all reference sources that provide different types of information. An encyclopedia provides short articles about topics, including people, places, events, and concepts. Dictionaries provide definitions and pronunciations of words. Almanacs provide lists of facts about many topics.

Nonfiction books can also serve as reference sources. In some reference sources, you may find a glossary, which defines terms found within the book. Many nonfiction books also have indexes that list general and specific topics in the book and page numbers where they can be found. You can find nonfiction books and other useful print sources by consulting the online catalog in your local library. If you enter a keyword, a title, or an author's name (last name first), the catalog will show all related books.

The library has a special section reserved for reference books such as encyclopedias, dictionaries, and almanacs. Usually, you cannot check out these books, but you can use them in the library. Many of these books will have a table of contents or index to help you find the information you need quickly. Don't be afraid to ask a librarian for assistance. They are there to help you find resources and information.

You can also find electronic or online versions of many reference sources by looking on the Internet. Most government, museum, and encyclopedia websites are reliable sources. However, many other resources on the Internet are not. By typing a keyword, title, or author into a search engine, you will receive hundreds, sometimes millions, of sources that have a range of reliability and relevance. It can be difficult to tell which sources provide legitimate information. Because they may have errors or a strong agenda, it is best to avoid personal websites, such as blogs, and websites that allow users to modify or add content.

Answer the questions.

> Suppose you want to find information about mountain climbing. How would you find reference sources? Which sources would you use?

You would enter *mountain climbing* into an online library catalog or a search engine. The library catalog would give you names of books about mountain climbing and their location in the library. The search engine would provide you with websites about mountain climbing. You could also look in a print or online encyclopedia.

Different reference books can help you research different types of information. The following list includes examples of reference materials and the type of information they provide.

encyclopedia	provides articles with facts about many topics
thesaurus	lists synonyms and antonyms for words
Books in Print	lists all currently in-print hardcover and paperback books by title, author, and subject
world atlas	provides maps and information about areas of the world
world almanac	provides facts about countries, weather, people, events, and many other topics
Guinness World Records	provides records that were set by people and events around the world
Bartlett's Familiar Quotations	lists famous quotations and the people who said them

List the reference source you would use to find the following information.

1. an antonym for the word *hardy*   _____

2. the author of a book if you know the title   _____

3. the population of India   _____

4. the location of the desert regions of Arizona   _____

5. the fastest waterskiing speed   _____

6. how clouds are formed   _____

7. the person who said "Early to bed, early to rise makes a man healthy, wealthy, and wise."   _____

8. what sharks eat   _____

9. how much rain fell in Missouri last year   _____

10. the world's largest popcorn ball   _____

11. a synonym for the word *silly*   _____

A glossary is an alphabetical list of terms that are found in a book. The glossary and index can be combined so you can reference pages in the book for more information.

Glossary/Index

Atmosphere: the envelope of gases and particles that surrounds Earth, held by the pull of gravity, *15–22, 188*

Barometer: an instrument that measures atmospheric pressure, *124–128*

Blizzard: heavy snow accompanied by winds of at least 35 miles per hour, *64, 68*

Climate: the pattern of weather that a location experiences over a specific period, *12, 15, 17*

Cloud: small liquid water droplets or ice crystals held in the atmosphere, *24–32, 65*

Convergence: an accumulation of air caused by air moving into the area from different directions, *34, 67*

Circle the letter of the answer to each question using the glossary/index above.

1. What is most likely the subject of the book that contains this glossary?

   A astronomy

   B weather

   C plants

   D animals

2. What is a weather condition that includes snow and strong winds?

   F blizzard

   G cloud

   H barometer

   J climate

3. On what page would you find information about climates?

   A page 17

   B page 26

   C page 68

   D page 124

4. Which of the following is a weather instrument?

   F cloud

   G convergence

   H atmosphere

   J barometer

5. Suppose the author wants to add the word *condensation* to the glossary. Which word would follow it?

   A climate

   B cloud

   C convergence

   D blizzard

6. On what page might you find information about how rain develops?

   F page 15

   G page 34

   H page 41

   J page 65

Use what you know about reference materials to circle the letter of the answer to each question.

1. Which website would provide the most reliable and relevant information about the migration of polar bears?

    A a website that is edited and written by its users

    B a science museum website

    C a polar bear discussion forum

    D a website where the author discusses his or her views about polar bears

2. You can find a book in the online library catalog by knowing the book's

    F publisher.

    G author.

    H year of publication.

    J number of pages.

3. Which term might be defined in the glossary of a cookbook?

    A astronomy

    B cross stitch

    C field goal

    D broil

4. Which term might be defined in the glossary of a book about baseball?

    F inning

    G trumpet

    H congress

    J harvest

5. Which reference source would you use to find out which person can hold his or her breath the longest?

    A encyclopedia

    B world atlas

    C *Guiness World Records*

    D *Bartlett's Familiar Quotations*

6. Which reference source would you use to find out the average rainfall in Ghana last year?

    F world almanac

    G *Books in Print*

    H thesaurus

    J *Guiness World Records*

Workplace Skill:
Use Reference Sources in an E-mail Attachment

The Allied Electrical Equipment Company is opening a new office and manufacturing plant in Brasilia, Brazil. It sent a company e-mail announcing the opening of the new office. It included an attachment to the e-mail. The attachment provides information and statistics of interest to employees who will be interacting with the new office.

Read the attachment. Then circle the letter of the answer to each question.

Allied Electrical Equipment Company
Office/Manufacturing Plant: Brasilia, Brazil

Brazil: About 80 percent of all Brazilians live within 200 miles of the Atlantic Coast. Nearly all of Brazil's big cities and towns are on or near the coast. Brazil is the largest country in South America in both area and population.

Population (2009): 191,971,506

Largest Cities:

São Paulo: 41,384,039
Rio de Janeiro: 16,010,429
Brasilia: 2,557,000 (capital of Brazil)

Official Language: Portuguese

Economy: Chief products: *Agriculture*—bananas, cacao beans, cassava, cattle, chickens, coffee. *Manufacturing and processing*—automobiles, cement, chemicals, electrical equipment. *Mining*—bauxite, coal, diamonds, gold, iron ore.

Climate: Most of the country has a warm to hot climate year-round.

Money: Basic unit—real. One hundred centavos equals one real.

Brasilia Time Zone: BET (Brazil Eastern Time)

Form of Government: Federal Republic

1. What would be the best source to use to locate where Brasilia is in comparison to São Paulo?

   A   a dictionary
   B   a world atlas
   C   a thesaurus
   D   a glossary

2. If you needed to fact-check the current population figures for Brazil, which is the best source to use?

   F   a blog site from Brazil
   G   a Brazilian government website
   H   a magazine article on economic trends
   J   a textbook on South American history

Write for Work

Your manager wants to add another attachment to the e-mail. He wants you to locate the following additional facts about Brasilia:

- How large is the city's geographic area?
- Where is the city located in Brazil?
- What ethnic groups are represented in the population?

Use appropriate reference sources to find the information. Write your attachment on Brasilia in a notebook. Include the reference sources you used.

 **Reading Extension**

Turn to "Death on the Unsinkable Titanic" on page 59 of *Reading Basics Intermediate 2 Reader*. After you have read and/or listened to the article, answer the questions below.

Circle the letter of the answer to each question.

1. Which reference source could you use to find out more information about the *Titanic*?
   - **A** a world almanac
   - **B** an online encyclopedia
   - **C** *Books in Print*
   - **D** a thesaurus

2. What word might be in the glossary of a book about the *Titanic*?
   - **F** iceberg
   - **G** parasol
   - **H** dolphin
   - **J** seaweed

Write the answer to each question.

3. Look in a thesaurus. What is a synonym for *titanic*?

_____

4. Smith wanted to prove that the *Titanic* was the fastest ship in the world. What resource could you use to find out what current ship holds that record?

_____

Explore Words

Plural nouns are "nouns that name more than one thing." Some words have plural forms that do not follow the usual rules. The plural form of some words is the same as the singular. For example: *One deer ran through the woods today. Yesterday, I saw two deer.*

Other words have plural forms that are completely different from the singular forms. For example: *My child goes to the King School. Where do your children go?*

Choose an irregular plural word to complete each sentence. Write the plural on the line.

Singular	Plural	Singular	Plural
tooth	teeth	sheep	sheep
mouse	mice	moose	moose
foot	feet	wheat	wheat
man	men	series	series
oasis	oases	salmon	salmon

1. That actor has been in several television _____.

2. How many _____ did you catch on your fishing trip?

3. I set out traps to catch the _____ in the kitchen.

4. We get wool from _____.

5. The dentist said I have cavities in a few _____.

Homophones are words that sound alike but are spelled differently and have different meanings. For example, *build* and *billed* are homophones.

Complete each sentence with one of the words in parentheses. Write the word on the line.

1. Please use this wooden _____ for the new bookcase. (board, bored)

2. You will need to fix the _____ in your car. (brakes, breaks)

3. Do the numbers in the report _____ accurate? (seam, seem)

4. My boss _____ me to leave early yesterday. (allowed, aloud)

SUFFIXES -ize, -ify

A suffix is a word part that you can add to the end of many words. Adding a suffix changes the meaning and sometimes the spelling of the word to which it is added. The suffixes -ize and -ify mean "to make or become." For example, *modernize* means "to make or become modern," and *purify* means "to make or become pure."

Write the base word for each word in the box. Then choose a word from the box to complete each sentence. Write the word on the line.

falsify _____	immunize _____	solidify _____
visualize _____	centralize _____	criminalize _____

1. I hope that they will _____ texting while driving.

2. A flu shot will _____ you against the flu.

3. It's a really bad idea to _____ your job experience.

4. All our offices are going to _____ in one building.

5. When you describe your hometown, I can _____ it in my mind.

6. The gelatin is beginning to _____ in the refrigerator.

ACADEMIC VOCABULARY

Knowing these high-frequency words will help you in many school subjects.

source   a book or document used to find facts in research

consult   to check a source to get or verify information

research the study of materials and sources to find facts and draw conclusions

general   not specific

index   an alphabetical list of topics and the pages on which they are found

Complete the sentences below using one of the words above.

1. Omar needed to _____ a dictionary to find the pronunciation of a word.

2. Makina didn't need details; she just needed _____ information.

3. Marietta cited the newspaper as the _____ of her information about rezoning.

4. Camisha looked in the _____ to find the pages that discussed marsupials.

5. Magi's _____ into the matter turned up some surprising information.

Lesson 2.4

Recognize Character Traits

INTRODUCE

People you know or read about and characters in novels or other literary works have character traits. Character traits are ways of behaving, beliefs, physical characteristics, and patterns of speech. Fiction authors use the following methods to show character traits. Writers of nonfiction use these same methods to show the traits of real people.

> **Narration:** The author tells how the character or real person looks, describes his or her inner thoughts or feelings, or tells what other characters think about him or her.

> **Dialogue:** The author tells what the character or real person says and how he or she says it. The author tells what others in the work say about him or her.

> **Action:** The author has the character or real person do things that reveal his or her personality.

Read the example and notice how the author shows character traits:

> Mimi went over to the bathroom door, drew back her right foot, and kicked the base of the door so savagely that the whole frame shook and pain shot up her leg.

You can determine that Mimi is angry and impulsive by the things she does. She violently kicks a door even though the action causes pain to her.

Read the passage. Identify examples of dialogue, narration, and action the author uses to tell that the woman is in a hurry.

> She was tall and graceful, wearing a blue suit and dark glasses. She carried several packages under her arm. She barely took notice of the people around her, so intent was she on getting where she was going. Nervously, she glanced at her watch as she walked down the street.
>
> Finally, she reached a long, black limousine. The driver leaped out and opened a door for her. "Okay, Niran," she said. "Let's get home before Tisa does. You know how impatient 10-year-olds can be."

Dialogue: "Let's get home before Tisa does."

Narration: The narrator tells us that the woman's focus is on getting where she is going.

Action: The woman glances at her watch nervously.

Read the passage. Then fill in the graphic organizer. In each box, write a word or phrase that describes Keisha.

Keisha worked a 12-hour overnight shift in the emergency room at the hospital. Working in the ER was exciting but exhausting. Early in the evening, an ambulance brought in a woman who fell while mountain climbing. The woman was bleeding a lot and crying, but Keisha remained composed as she spent four hours cleaning and stitching the woman's head and mangled leg. The woman was frightened and in pain, so Keisha kept reassuring the woman that she would be okay and that the pain would subside.

Now, Keisha was dragging her tired body the four blocks to her home where she could take off her shoes and crawl into bed. Just then, out of the corner of her eye, Keisha spotted Mrs. De La Rosa across the street, carrying a bag of groceries and pushing a stroller. Keisha rushed over. "Can I carry that for you?" she asked.

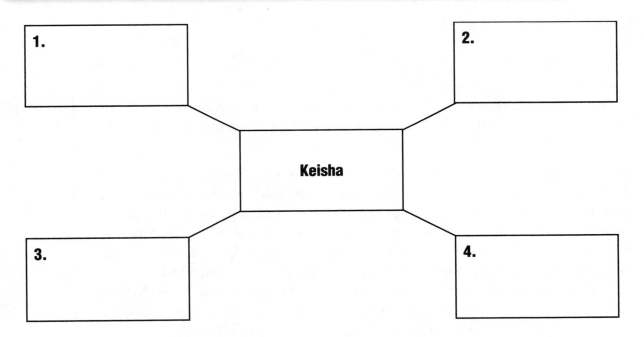

1.

2.

Keisha

3.

4.

Write two methods the author used to tell you what Keisha was like. For each method, list one or more examples from the passage.

5. _____

_____

6. _____

_____

Read each passage. Then answer each question.

Calixto groaned when the car commercial with the horrible jingle came on. He hit mute and pulled out his phone, looking for new text messages. Eventually, the commercial ended, and he turned the sound back on. He really didn't like the show that was on, but if he kept watching, he wouldn't have to think of anything better to do. He picked up a bag of potato chips from where he had set it on the floor and shoveled some into his mouth, wiping the greasy residue on his pants. He was thirsty, but he had finished his soda and didn't feel like walking to the store to buy more. He picked up a magazine and flipped through it, keeping one ear on the show he didn't like and the other waiting for the beep that signaled new messages.

1. Who is the main character in this passage? _____

2. What two words could describe him? _____

3. What method or methods did the author use to reveal these traits?

_____

"It would be a fine morning," Steve thought, "if Miss MacGill would stop watching me through the gas station window." As he pumped gas for a customer, he could see her over his shoulder always watching him.

Steve bent down, checking the flow of gas from the nozzle. There was a gas shortage going on, and he'd been hearing talk about rationing new customers. If he spilled a drop, she would be after him. Not that it mattered because she was always after him about something. Yesterday she had bawled him out when the air pump stopped working in the afternoon. A woman had left the pump on, and it had used too much electricity. Steve said he would pay for the extra electricity, and Miss MacGill said she would dock his Saturday pay. "That's bad enough," thought Steve, "but I don't like the way she just sits there and stares, trying to catch me doing something wrong. If I could, I'd quit right now and never come back."

4. Who are the characters in this passage? _____

5. What two words could describe Miss MacGill? _____

6. What method or methods were used to reveal these traits?

_____

Read each passage. Then circle the letter of the answer to each question.

As I walked along 10th Street, I noticed a small store squeezed in between two huge brick buildings. The sign in red letters across the window said DANDY'S CANDY STORE. I sidestepped a kid whose dirty little fingers were busy tearing off the wrapper that hid his candy bar. I knew I needed something sweet and delicious, so I went inside and found my favorite type of candy bar. I was barely out the door before I'd eaten the whole thing.

I rolled the wrapper from my candy bar between my palms into a tiny ball. I made a basketball from it and threw it toward an overflowing garbage can. It landed on the edge and fell to the sidewalk. I picked it up, partly because I didn't want to add to the mess on the pavement and partly because it's not cool to miss an easy basket.

1. Which best describes the main character?
- **A** fearless and sly
- **B** lazy and afraid
- **C** relaxed and easygoing
- **D** foolish and thoughtless

2. What method(s) does the author use to develop the character?
- **F** narration and actions
- **G** actions
- **H** dialogue
- **J** narration and dialogue

John Fleming took off his raincoat and hung it on a peg behind the door. Then he took off his tweed jacket and hung it next to the raincoat. He put on the woolen cardigan that he wore at the office. One of its leather buttons was missing, a lone string hanging from what used to be its spot. He pushed his hair back with a hand and nervously bit the knuckle of his right thumb.

3. Which is a character trait of John Fleming?
- **A** He spends a lot of money on clothes.
- **B** He is sick.
- **C** He dresses to impress others.
- **D** He is worried.

4. How do you learn about the character?
- **F** through the words of others
- **G** through the character's actions
- **H** through his thoughts
- **J** through dialogue

Workplace Skill: Match Character Traits in a Job Description

What character traits—the particular qualities of a person—do companies look for in potential employees? Certain jobs require people with certain character traits. A job description identifies and spells out the responsibilities of a specific job. It can also provide an idea of what special characteristics a person should have to accomplish the job successfully. The Town of Riverside has placed the following job description on the Riverside Community Bulletin Board.

Read the description. Then circle the letter of the answer to each question.

Community Green Initiative Planner

Job Description:

The Town of Riverside is looking for a Community Green Initiative Planner. He or she will develop and implement comprehensive community greening projects and programs. The job requires a high degree of professionalism, sensitivity, and integrity. This person will also be responsible for enhancing the public profile of the town. Working effectively with community leaders, environmental and civic groups, and other community organizations will be important.

Key responsibilities include:

- Foster a local awareness of the benefits of green planning projects for the community through public information campaigns and activities.
- Develop and oversee public events to promote active lifestyles using local public space, such as the annual "Breathe Green" Block Party.
- Create a community greening projects pipeline.
- Work with local students to develop green projects in local schools.

Requirements:

- Bachelor's degree in city and regional planning
- 2+ years of experience
- Strong familiarity with tree maintenance and green building technologies
- Clear vision on green development and ability to motivate people

---

1. To be able to "motivate people" effectively, what character traits would be useful for a candidate for this position to have?

  A confidence and enthusiasm

  B neatness and orderliness

  C patience and helpfulness

  D seriousness and stubbornness

2. Which action shows the character trait of sensitivity?

  F organizing the workspace

  G listening to the views of others

  H bossing people around

  J criticizing others' ideas

Write for Work

You are applying for the position of Community Green Initiative Planner. List the character traits that would help a prospective employee to be successful in this position. In a notebook, write a paragraph explaining how your special character traits match the character traits needed for this position.

 **Reading Extension**

Turn to "Sarah's Ghost House: An Architectural Fun House" on page 68 of *Reading Basics Intermediate 2 Reader*. After you have read and/or listened to the article, answer the questions below.

Circle the letter of the answer to each question.

1. What are Sarah's character traits?

   A laziness and greed

   B laziness and fear

   C fear and superstition

   D superstition and greed

2. What method(s) does the writer use to reveal these traits?

   F narration and action

   G action and dialogue

   H dialogue and narration

   J action alone

3. Which character trait do Sarah's servants show by their refusal to say whether the ghosts' food and drink had been touched?

   A discretion

   B gossip

   C ignorance

   D idleness

Write the answer to each question.

4. What is one way the author shows that Sarah really believed in the ghosts?

_____

5. What does the author reveal by listing all the uses of the number 13 in the house?

_____

Explore Words

A syllable is a word part with one vowel sound. A closed syllable ends with a consonant and usually has a short vowel sound. An open syllable ends with a vowel and usually has a long vowel sound. A silent *e* syllable ends with a silent *e* and usually has a long vowel sound. Consonant + *le* syllables usually occur at the end of words.

Match each syllable from Column A with a syllable from Column B to form a word. Write the new word on the line. If the first syllable has a long vowel sound, underline it once. If it has a short vowel sound, underline it twice.

	Column A	Column B	
1.	ro	ple	_____
2.	cab	gle	_____
3.	sim	tate	_____
4.	in	sell	_____
5.	bu	in	_____
6.	re	vite	_____

The following groups of syllables are scrambled. Put each group in order to form a three-syllable word. Then write the word. The first item has been done for you.

7. tan un gle _____*untangle*_____   **9.** vent ed pre _____

8. nect con dis _____   **10.** tas fan tic _____

A prefix is a word part that you can add to the beginning of many words. Adding a prefix changes the meaning of the word to which it is added. The prefix *in-* can mean "not." For example, *incorrect* means "not correct." The prefix *dis-* means "not" or "the opposite of." For example, *dishonest* means "not honest."

Use the prefix *in-* or *dis-* to write a word with the meaning given. Write the word on the line.

1. not direct _____   **4.** not like _____

2. not sane _____   **5.** the opposite of agreement _____

3. the opposite of order _____   **6.** the opposite of obey _____

Some words have more than one meaning. For example, a *table* is a piece of furniture. Used another way, *table* also means "to postpone or put aside," as in "to *table* a decision." You can use context clues—other words in the same sentence or nearby sentences—to figure out which meaning is intended.

Use context clues in each sentence that help you know the intended meaning of the underlined word. Circle the letter of the intended meaning.

1. She wanted to <u>express</u> her gratitude.

    a. to show or communicate

    b. fast or direct

2. The seller will <u>counter</u> any offer you make.

    a. a flat surface in a kitchen

    b. to act in response

3. Do you have any <u>interest</u> in traveling?

    a. a charge made on a loan

    b. curiosity or desire

4. My grandfather plays the <u>organ</u> in church.

    a. a musical instrument

    b. a part of the body

5. I made a <u>pitcher</u> of lemonade.

    a. a container that holds liquids

    b. a position on a baseball team

6. There are many sailboats on the <u>sound</u>.

    a. a noise

    b. a body of water

7. The <u>light</u> from the lamp cast a shadow.

    a. pale, not dark in color

    b. a source of illumination

8. She is wearing a new <u>jumper</u> today.

    a. someone who jumps

    b. a type of dress

Knowing these high-frequency words will help you in many school subjects.

characters	people in novels and other literary works
traits	the things about people that make them special
method	a particular way of doing something
reveal	to make information known to others
focus	concentrating activity or interest on something

Complete the sentences below using one of the words above.

1. The _____ in the play seemed as complicated as any real people.

2. Carol ignored the ringing phone. She kept her _____ on driving.

3. Zuri's _____ of locating information was very effective.

4. The writer waited until the end of the book to _____ the killer's identity.

5. The _____ most people associated with her were kindness and caring.

Lesson 2.5

Use Supporting Evidence

When writers make a statement or express an opinion in writing, they usually support it with evidence. Supporting evidence, which is additional information that helps prove a point or that gives weight to an opinion, may appear as facts, statistics, examples, or reasons.

Regardless of whether the main idea is a fact or an opinion, evaluate the details in a passage to determine whether these details act as supporting evidence. Some details may not support the main idea in the way the writer intended. There may also be details that negate or contradict the main idea. Additionally, there may be unrelated details that neither support nor contradict the main idea. When you analyze a passage to find supporting evidence for the main idea, you must eliminate unrelated or contradictory details. Then you can judge whether the details that remain are strong enough to back up the writer's point.

Read the example. The main idea appears in boldfaced type, and the supporting evidence is underlined.

> **In nature, there are patterns that repeat.** <u>One example is the seasons of the year. Another example is the phases of the moon.</u> Can you name some others?

The evidence in the example above supports the main idea. They are facts that give examples of patterns that repeat in nature.

Read the passage. Circle the main idea. Then underline the sentences that provide supporting evidence.

> Born in 1867 in Lake Pepin, Wisconsin, Laura Ingalls Wilder first lived in a log cabin. The cabin was located at the edge of a large woods. Later she moved with her family to Kansas, Minnesota, and the Dakota Territory, among other places. Laura Ingalls Wilder spent her early life in the American Midwest.

Did you circle the last sentence? It tells the main idea of the passage, that Wilder lived in places throughout the Midwest. The first sentence supports it. The first sentence tells that Wilder was born in Wisconsin, which is part of the Midwest. The other sentence that acts as supporting evidence is, "Later she moved with her family to Kansas, Minnesota, and the Dakota Territory, among other places." This sentence names other places in the Midwest where Wilder lived.

Read the passage. Then circle the letter of the answer to each question.

Paper and movable type were first known in China, but printing was first mechanized in Europe. The idea of the printing press was modeled on the wine and olive presses used in Mediterranean countries. Mediterranean countries are known for their selection of olives. The flatbed wooden printing press could print about 250 sheets per hour on one side. This invention lasted for more than three centuries. Metal cylinder presses came into use in the late 1700s. Furthermore, about this time people considered using steam to power the presses. Steam already powered many kinds of inventions, including some engines. The new steam presses were much faster, producing 8,000 sheets per hour.

1. What is the main idea of this passage?

   A   China invented paper and movable type.

   B   Mechanized printing has evolved over the centuries.

   C   The printing press was modeled on wine and olive presses.

   D   Printing presses powered by steam were faster than older presses.

2. Which sentence does NOT support the main idea?

   F   This invention lasted for more than three centuries.

   G   Metal cylinder presses came into use in the late 1700s.

   H   Mediterranean countries are known for their selection of olives.

   J   The new steam presses were much faster, producing 8,000 sheets per hour.

3. Which sentence could be added to the passage to support the main idea?

   A   Today, artists can study a technique called printmaking.

   B   Engraved printing is very expensive and highly prized in formal stationery.

   C   The Linotype machine was invented in the late 1800s and made it easier to set moveable type for printing.

   D   The electric typewriter was invented in 1872 by Thomas Edison, but James Smathers developed the use of the machine in offices 50 years later.

4. How is the supporting evidence related to the main idea?

   F   The supporting evidence gives examples of some advances in mechanized printing presses.

   G   The supporting evidence shows that printed works are easier to read and reproduce than handwritten works.

   H   The supporting evidence explains how mechanized printing led to greater literacy.

   J   The supporting evidence describes the most modern kinds of printing presses.

For each main idea, give two examples of supporting evidence that might appear in a passage along with that main idea.

Birds build their nests in unusual places.

1. _____

_____

2. _____

_____

Washington, D.C., has many places of historical interest.

3. _____

_____

4. _____

_____

The most crucial factor in making good pizza is the ingredients.

5. _____

_____

6. _____

_____

Making a schedule will help you finish things on time.

7. _____

_____

8. _____

_____

Read the passage. Then circle the letter of the answer to each question.

(1) International trade benefits economies. (2) Because of trade, firms in different countries can produce goods that are most suited to their resources. (3) For example, Brazil's soil and climate are suited to the production of coffee, while the soil and climate in the United States favor corn. (4) If each country produces products in which it has a natural advantage, total output rises. (5) Surplus crops can be sold to other countries. (6) Trade also promotes competition, which helps create new technologies, products, and businesses.

1. What is the main idea of this passage?

  A International trade benefits economies.

  B Trade promotes competition, which helps create new technologies, products, and businesses.

  C If each country produces products in which it has a natural advantage, total output rises.

  D Because of trade, firms in different countries can produce goods that are most suited to their resources.

2. Which sentence could be added to the passage to act as additional supporting evidence for the main idea?

  F Many people prefer to purchase things made or grown in their own country.

  G International trade allows consumers more choice in the goods they buy.

  H Import and export tariffs are often levied on international sales.

  J It is difficult to order things from another country.

3. How does the following sentence act as supporting evidence for the main idea?

  Surplus crops can be sold to other countries.

  A It gives statistics on how economies have improved by trading internationally.

  B It acts as an example of one way in which economies can benefit.

  C It is the opinion of an expert in the field of international trade.

  D It does not act as supporting evidence.

4. Which sentence provides specific examples to act as supporting evidence?

  F sentence 1

  G sentence 2

  H sentence 3

  J sentence 4

Workplace Skill: Find Supporting Evidence in a Leave-of-absence Policy

Company policies contain important information for employees and should be read carefully. The purpose of company policies is to inform employees and to set uniform treatment and instruction.

Read the leave-of-absence policy. Then circle the letter of the answer to each question.

Carter Preschool
Medical Leave-of-absence Policy

Carter Preschool prides itself on meeting the needs of its children, teaching staff, and their families. A serious medical condition may arise during your employment. That condition may prevent you from working for more than 10 consecutive school days. In that case, you may take a medical leave of absence from your job.

Teachers and aides who take a medical leave of absence may be asked to do the following:

- Obtain a medical evaluation from their primary-care physician.
- Complete the forms required by the school department.
- Obtain a physician's release note upon returning to school.

If a medical condition develops, you must notify the director as soon as possible. You must maintain contact with her throughout your absence. If your absence will exceed 10 consecutive days, your director may need to arrange for temporary coverage by a substitute teacher. Your cooperation with and advance notice of (when possible) such absences is greatly appreciated. This leave of absence may be extended for up to one year. It is available to full-time staff after six months of employment.

1. What is the main idea of the policy?

   A A medical leave of absence is for more than 10 consecutive workdays

   B Staff members need a physician's release on returning to school

   C The preschool is grateful for advance notice of an absence

   D School staff need to follow the guidelines described in the policy in order to take a medical leave of absence

2. Which sentence is not an example of supporting evidence or details?

   F You may be required to obtain a medical evaluation from your primary-care physician.

   G You may need to complete a form required by the school department.

   H Carter Preschool prides itself on meeting the needs of its children, teaching staff, and their families.

   J You may need to obtain a physician's release note upon returning to school.

Write for Work

Imagine that you have landed your dream job. You are excited and want to write or e-mail a friend about it. First, in a notebook, write the key responsibility of the job you have been offered. Then list three details that support the key responsibility.

 **Reading Extension**

Turn to "Krakatoa: The Doomsday Crack Heard 'Round the World" on page 78 of *Reading Basics Intermediate 2 Reader*. After you have read and/or listened to the article, answer the questions below.

Circle the letter of the answer to each question.

1. What is the main idea of paragraph 5?
   - **A** The volcano's light volcanic ash and dust rose into the atmosphere, where winds carried it all over the Earth.
   - **B** Weather all over the planet was affected for months after the eruption.
   - **C** For two years, the reflection of the sun on the ash in the upper atmosphere resulted in spectacular sunsets.
   - **D** The skies over the United States glowed so red that people thought the color was the result of gigantic fires.

2. What is the main type of supporting evidence that the author uses in paragraph 5?
   - **F** statistics
   - **G** examples
   - **H** opinions
   - **J** quotes from experts

3. What was the only living thing to survive the eruption on Krakatoa?
   - **A** a red spider
   - **B** grass
   - **C** a tree
   - **D** a shrub

Write the answer to the question.

4. Do you think the author's evidence is enough to support the idea that the eruption on Krakatoa influenced weather all over the world? Why? _____

_____

Explore Words

Possessive words show that something belongs to one person or more than one person. Singular possessive words include an apostrophe followed by s ('s). For example, the office where one friend works is *your friend's office*. Most plural possessive words include an s followed by an apostrophe (s'). For example, the office where two or more of your friends work is *your friends' office*.

Show ownership by writing a possessive phrase. Use 's or s'.

1. the collar that belongs to the dog _____

2. the teacher that your daughter has _____

3. the children of your sister _____

4. the party that my cousins gave _____

5. the lunch that Suchin brought _____

SPELLING: WORD ENDINGS

You can add the endings *-ed* and *-ing* to the end of many verbs to change the form. When you add *-ed* or *-ing*, remember these spelling rules:

- When a word ends with silent *e*, drop the *e*. Then add *-ed* or *-ing*.

    manage   manag<u>ed</u>   manag<u>ing</u>

- When a word ends in a consonant followed by *y*, change the *y* to *i*. Then add *-ed*. Do not change the spelling to add *-ing*.

    carr<u>y</u>   carr<u>ied</u>   carr<u>ing</u>

    tr<u>y</u>   tr<u>ied</u>   try<u>ing</u>.

Add the ending to each word. Write the new word on the line.

1. supply + ed   _____   **6.** underline + ed   _____

2. rely + ing   _____   **7.** profile + ing   _____

3. suppose + ed   _____   **8.** ready + ing   _____

4. study + ing   _____   **9.** reunite + ing   _____

5. donate + ing   _____   **10.** explode + ed   _____

LATIN ROOTS

A root contains the main meaning of a word but cannot stand alone. Many words in English combine Latin roots with prefixes and suffixes or other endings. Here are some common Latin roots and their meanings.

Root	Meaning	Root	Meaning
port	carry	*voc*	call or voice
ject	throw	*vis* or *vid*	see

For each word in the left column, underline the root and think about the meaning. Then choose the correct definition from the right column. Write the letter on the line.

_____ 1. revision

_____ 2. portable

_____ 3. rejection

_____ 4. importer

_____ 5. visor

_____ 6. vocation

_____ 7. projector

a. one who brings items into a country

b. a special calling

c. equipment that throws an image onto a screen

d. a change made after looking again

e. being tossed off or refused

f. able to be carried

g. something that protects the eyes

ACADEMIC VOCABULARY

Knowing these high-frequency words will help you in many school subjects.

evidence information or facts that show whether something is true

support to suggest that something is true or endorse it

statistics a collection of quantitative data

example something that illustrates a general rule

eliminate to remove or get rid of

Complete the sentences below using one of the words above.

1. The pitcher's _____ showed he had the best win/loss record in his division.

2. Sanura made her best case, but there was no _____ to back up her opinion.

3. Mealea was glad the instructions included an _____ for her to follow.

4. Orilio's strategy was to _____ some of the incorrect answer choices.

5. The report was rejected because the writer did not _____ his conclusions.

Lesson 2.6

Identify Author's Purpose

Everything you read was written for a reason. Authors typically write for one or more of the following purposes: to persuade, to inform, to explain, to entertain, or to describe.

- When the purpose is to persuade, the author may present facts and opinions that he or she thinks will make the reader come to a certain conclusion.
- When the purpose is to inform, the author gives information about a subject.
- When the purpose is to explain, the author might give instructions for how to do something or give details telling why something happens.
- When the purpose is to entertain, the author may use humor, suspense, or details with a high interest level.
- When the purpose is to describe, the author creates a picture using words.

Ask yourself the following questions to understand the author's purpose for writing: *Is the author making an argument? Is this piece funny, suspenseful, or otherwise entertaining? Is the author teaching me something?*

Authors sometimes have more than one purpose in mind for a particular piece of writing. For example, an entertaining piece can also persuade, and a descriptive piece can also inform. However, most writers have a primary purpose for writing about a particular subject. As you read, try to determine the author's purpose or purposes for writing. Knowing this can help you interpret what you read. Read the following example that was written to describe a place called Easton:

> Tangy sea breezes drift through Easton. Vacationers love Easton's grassy parks and seaside play.

The writer uses expressive language to describe a setting, and the details in the example paint a picture of the place.

Read the passage. What is the author's primary purpose?

> With just a few adjustments in your lifestyle, you can reduce your water bill and help conserve an important natural resource. Remember to turn off the faucet when you brush your teeth, shave, or wash dishes. Incorporate a basin as part of these activities and run the water only for the last step. In addition, purchase a special showerhead that releases a limited amount of water.

The author's purpose is to explain how to save water.

Match each form of writing in column 1 with a purpose from column 2. Write the letter on the line.

1. an adventure story _____   **a.** to persuade

2. a letter to the editor _____   **b.** to entertain

3. a recipe _____   **c.** to explain or instruct

4. a travel brochure _____   **d.** to inform

5. a news story _____   **e.** to describe

Read each passage. Then write the purpose or purposes that the author may have had for writing the passage.

to entertain	to inform	to describe	to explain or instruct	to persuade

Many sounds are common to a large number of languages. Nevertheless, languages do not all have the same sounds or the same number of sounds. This can make it challenging to learn a new language.

6. _____

I had walked a few miles along the dunes when I noticed dark clouds rolling in. Suddenly there came a clap of thunder. It was an angry, metallic sound. A mighty wind arose and filled the air with dust. Palm trees swayed, and the birds were silent.

7. _____

Of all the travel magazines on the market today, the one I recommend is *Hit the Road*. Interesting articles about exotic destinations will grab your attention and make your reading an enjoyable experience.

8. _____

Read the scenarios. Identify what the person will write and for what purpose: to entertain, to inform, to persuade or express an opinion, to describe, or to explain or instruct.

At the picnic, people compliment Mrs. Rodriguez on her taco salad. They ask her how to make the dish. What might Mrs. Rodriguez write and for what purpose?

1. She will write _____.

2. Her purpose for writing is _____.

Kamika's boss asks her to research three different recycling pick-up companies and compare their prices and features.

3. She will write _____.

4. Her purpose for writing is _____.

Ms. Nguyen is irate as she reads the local paper. The town council plans to raise taxes, and no one seems to be complaining or to understand that there are reasons that an increase would be difficult for some people.

5. She will write _____.

6. Her purpose for writing is _____.

Chaske wants to be a stand-up comedian, and the upcoming community talent show would give him an opportunity to practice his skill.

7. He will write _____.

8. His purpose for writing is _____.

Kaleb's favorite state is Wisconsin. He visits the state often and is asked by a local newspaper to write what can be seen there during each season of the year.

9. He will write _____.

10. His purpose for writing is _____.

In history class, Kenji was asked to choose a favorite historical person from the 20th century and to write about that person.

11. He will write _____.

12. His purpose for writing is _____.

Read each passage. Then circle the letter of the answer that shows the author's purpose for writing each passage.

The most famous leader during this time was Charles the Great, or Charlemagne. Pope Leo III crowned Charlemagne as the Holy Roman Emperor in A.D. 800. Charlemagne's title suggests that the Roman Empire still existed, but that empire had ended several hundred years earlier.

1. A to entertain   **C** to persuade

    B to inform   **D** to describe

She wasn't afraid of Black Diamond even if he was a rather high-strung and nervous horse. He was used to living in the wild, so it would all take time, but Dalila knew this when she made the bet with her father. He gave her three days to make friends with the horse and one month after that to ride him around the corral.

2. F to entertain   **H** to inform

    G to persuade   **J** to explain or instruct

Are you packing for a trip? No matter if you are going on a weekend trip or a month-long excursion, there are certain steps to follow when you pack your bags. First, place everything you want to bring on your bed. Then, take the largest items such as sweaters and jeans. Roll them as tightly as possible. Place the rolled items in the suitcase. Next, find smaller items such as t-shirts and swimsuits that will fit between the larger items. If you have to bring an extra pair of shoes, stuff the shoes with socks. Always place your toiletries in a sealed bag to prevent leaks.

3. A to entertain   **C** to persuade

    B to describe   **D** to explain or instruct

The towering, twisted tree stood weirdly on rows of long, skinny legs. It was a strangler fig, the strangest tree in the forest, and possibly the most important. It teemed with life of all kinds inside the nooks and crevices created by its many twisting trunks.

4. F to entertain   **H** to describe

    G to persuade   **J** to explain or instruct

Workplace Skill: Find Author's Purpose in a Business E-mail Memo

Businesses use memos to give information about company plans and policies. They also use memos to describe company procedures. Sometimes they use memos to persuade employees to act in a certain way. To identify the author's purpose for writing the memo, ask yourself what the author wants you to think, do, or feel as a result of reading it.

Read the memo. Then circle the letter of the answer to each question below the box.

From: Pamela Chen, Sunville Property Management
Date: September 22
To: All Residents of Two Siesta Park Plaza
Subject: Installation of Speed Tables

Due to an increasing concern regarding speeding in the parking lots at Two Siesta Park Plaza, speed tables will be installed in the parking lots on Thursday, October 7. This work has been scheduled to start at 7:00 A.M. and is expected to be completed by the end of the workday.

During construction, these areas may be inaccessible. Affected areas will be blocked off. Employees will have to find parking in other lots if their lot is blocked off.

One speed table will be installed at the pedestrian entrance to the parking garage; another will be installed at the rear walkway of Two Siesta Office Park.

We apologize for any inconvenience this may cause. As a reminder, please urge your employees to drive slowly in the parking lots.

Please feel free to contact Property Management at 701-555-9999 should you have any questions or concerns.

Thank you,

Pamela Chen
Tenant Coordinator
Sunville Property Management

---

1. What is the author's purpose in the e-mail memo?

   A to inform and to entertain

   B to persuade and to entertain

   C to inform and to persuade

   D to describe and to entertain

2. Which sentence tries to convince you to do something?

   F Affected areas will be blocked off.

   G Please urge your employees to drive slowly in the parking lots.

   H During construction, these areas may be inaccessible.

   J One speed table will be installed at the pedestrian entrance to the parking garage.

Write for Work

Imagine you are a tenant at Two Siesta Park Plaza and your company has received the e-mail memo on page 122. Your supervisor has asked you to write a memo to all employees to stress the importance of driving slowly in the parking lots to avoid accidents. Write your e-mail memo in a notebook.

Workplace Extension

Understanding Body Language

Rashid's boss has called him into her office unexpectedly. She wants to discuss the upcoming presentation they will both give on the last quarter's sales figures. Rashid has compiled most of the information he will need for his presentation and feels he is ready. Rashid, however, is preoccupied because he is afraid he will be late for a yoga class after work. He checks his watch often and looks down instead of making eye contact with his boss. Rashid is not aware of it, but he continuously taps his fingers on the chair. He hopes his boss will hurry up so he can make his yoga class. His boss keeps talking about how they should present the key issues in the presentation. Rashid slouches in his chair and crosses his arms over his chest.

Circle the letter of the answer to each question.

1. What impression will Rashid's boss probably take away from this meeting?

   A Rashid is an important and serious member of the staff.

   B Rashid is bored and not interested in the presentation.

   C Rashid likes and admires his boss.

   D Rashid is eager and ready for the presentation.

2. What kind of attitude is Rashid expressing in his nonverbal communication?

   F a positive attitude

   G a carefree attitude

   H a negative attitude

   J a cooperative attitude

Write the answer to the question.

3. What are some of the gestures that Rashid should have avoided in the meeting with his boss?

   _____

   _____

   _____

Explore Words

Different spellings sometimes stand for the same sound. For example, the letter *f* stands for the sound you hear at the beginning of *finish*. That same sound is represented by the letters *ph* in *phone* and *elephant* and the letters *gh* in *laugh* and *cough*.

Look at each word. If it is spelled correctly, write *correct* on the line. If it is not spelled correctly, rewrite the word with the correct spelling. Use a dictionary if you are not sure.

1. nephew _____   **5.** enouph _____

2. phences _____   **6.** feather _____

3. rephrain _____   **7.** alfabet _____

4. tough _____   **8.** gharmacy _____

WORD FAMILIES

A word family is a group of words that have the same base word. For example, *imagination*, *imaginary*, and *unimaginable* belong to the same word family. They each have the base word *imagine*.

Read each clue. Then circle the word that matches the clue.

1. able to decide easily

decisive   indecisive   deciding

2. not having the ability to create

creative   creation   uncreative

3. one who assists

assistance   assisting   assistant

ANTONYMS

Antonyms are words that have the opposite or almost the opposite meanings. For example, *true* and *false* are antonyms.

Find a word in each row that is an antonym for the first word. Circle the antonym.

1. accept   except   refuse   take

2. depart   arrive   leave   stay

3. private   secret   public   unknown

PREFIXES *inter-*, *semi-*, *multi-*

A prefix is a word part that can be added to the beginning of many words. Adding a prefix changes the meaning of a word to which it is added. For example, the prefix *un-* means "not" or "the opposite of," so the word *unnecessary* means "not necessary." Here are some other common prefixes, their meanings, and examples:

inter-	"between" or "among"	*intercoastal* (between coasts)
semi-	"partly" or "half"	*semisolid* (partly solid)
multi-	"many"	*multipurpose* (having many purposes)

Read each phrase. Add a prefix to the word in parentheses to create a word with the same meaning as the phrase. Write the new word on the line.

1. having many cultures: _____ (cultural)

2. between states: _____ (state)

3. half conscious: _____ (conscious)

4. between nations: _____ (national)

5. partly private: _____ (private)

6. having many levels: _____ (level)

ACADEMIC VOCABULARY

Knowing these high-frequency words will help you in many school subjects.

author   the person who writes something

purpose   the reason something is done

persuade   to convince someone to do something

inform   to give facts or information

explain   to make something clear by providing details, facts, or ideas.

Complete the sentences below using one of the words above.

1. The _____ of the trip was to meet with clients and investors.

2. The article did not _____ the problem very clearly, and many people were confused.

3. The hostess came to _____ us that our table was ready.

4. The _____ of the book signed copies at the bookstore event.

5. She tried to _____ her boss to give her an extra day off.

Unit 2 Review

Identify Sequence

The order in which events take place is called *sequence*. When you read, it is important to understand what happens first, second, third, and so on. Look for clue words such as *first, next, then*, and *last*. You also need to understand sequence to correctly follow directions.

Understand Consumer Materials

Consumer materials are documents that are written for consumers of products or services. These materials include advertisements, coupons, product labels, instructions, manuals, and forms related to services. These materials contain critical information, which consumers need to read carefully and understand.

Use Reference Sources

The library and the Internet are filled with reference sources that give you important information about almost any topic. Some sources are reliable, but many are not. It is important to know how to access information and evaluate sources for their reliability.

Recognize Character Traits

Characters in fiction and people in real life have character traits—ways of acting and speaking, beliefs, feelings, and physical characteristics. Authors of fiction and writers of nonfiction use methods such as narration, dialogue, and action to show character traits.

Use Supporting Evidence

When you express an opinion or state a main idea in writing, you must support it with evidence. Some details may be interesting but not related. Think carefully about what you are trying to say. Then include detailed evidence that supports your ideas.

Identify Author's Purpose

Authors typically write for one or more of the following purposes: to persuade, to inform, to explain, to entertain, or to describe. Identifying the author's primary purpose helps readers to interpret what they read.

Unit 2 Assessment

Read each passage. Then circle the letter of the answer to each question.

> The first mission to land people on the moon was Apollo 11. The spacecraft blasted off on July 16, 1969, with astronauts Neil Armstrong, Edwin E. Aldrin, Jr., and Michael Collins aboard. For three days, they coasted toward the moon. Once in lunar orbit, Armstrong and Aldrin separated the lunar module, *Eagle*, from the command/service module, *Columbia*, and began the landing maneuver. Armstrong chose a lowland as the *Eagle*'s landing site. On July 20, 1969, he radioed back the famous announcement "Houston, Tranquility Base here. The *Eagle* has landed." After landing, the astronauts put on space suits, opened a small hatch, and stepped onto the moon. After collecting rocks and soil samples and setting up automatic science equipment, they returned to *Columbia* for the return trip to Earth. *Columbia* splashed down into the Pacific Ocean on July 24.

1. What was the first thing that happened after Apollo 11 blasted off?

   A The spacecraft coasted toward the moon.

   B The astronauts collected rock samples.

   C The astronauts put on space suits.

   D The spacecraft went into lunar orbit.

2. What was the author's primary purpose for writing this paragraph?

   F to explain how the Apollo 11 spacecraft worked

   G to persuade readers to support the U.S. space program

   H to describe the Apollo 11 mission

   J to entertain readers with a suspenseful story about space

> The Statue of Liberty, which stands in New York Harbor, was a present from the people of France to the people of the United States. The enormous statue is a figure of a woman holding a torch. The statue measures 151 feet from its base to the top of the torch, and it weighs 225 tons. The torch, which the woman holds in her right hand, is a symbol of enlightenment. The statue is covered in copper sheeting that's about the thickness of two pennies. It stands on a granite-covered concrete pedestal that is an additional 154 feet high.

3. The author's primary purpose for writing this paragraph was

   A to persuade people to visit the Statue of Liberty.

   B to inform readers about the location of the Statue of Liberty.

   C to explain all the symbols represented in the Statue of Liberty.

   D to describe the Statue of Liberty.

4. Which reference source would you use to find out more information about the Statue of Liberty?

   F a world almanac

   G a thesaurus

   H an atlas

   J an encyclopedia

When honeybees fly about in a garden, they may appear to flutter aimlessly from one flower to the next. Most people don't know why bees choose one flower over another, but the bees themselves know why. In fact, when on a mission to find nectar, they follow an internal timetable to get the maximum amount of the sweet stuff. Bees tend to gather nectar from dandelions in the morning. After that, they may visit the cornflowers, and shortly after noon, the bees might set off for red clover.

5. When do the honeybees get nectar from cornflowers?

   A before the dandelions

   B after the red clover

   C some time around noon

   D late in the evening

6. Which sentence would act as additional supporting evidence for the main idea of the paragraph?

   F After the red clover, honeybees might get nectar from apple blossoms.

   G Honeybee behavior has always been a mystery to scientists.

   H There appears to be no pattern to honeybee behavior.

   J Honeybees use nectar to make honey in the hive.

Carmelita paced restlessly at the edge of the field, watching her teammates scurry up and down the soccer field. Time was running out for the exhausted players, but they were two goals behind. "I know we can beat the other team," murmured Carmelita, clenching and unclenching her hands. Carmelita glanced over at the coach, silently begging to be put into the game. Coach Cruz shook his head as he sighed and said, "Do whatever you can, Carmelita, but it doesn't look too good." Carmelita bolted onto the field with a whoop and shouted encouragement to her tired teammates. Immediately, she cornered the ball and raced down the field before her opponents even had time to catch their breaths. In the next instant, she narrowed the gap to one goal. Carmelita had breathed new life into her dragging team, so she gathered the players into a huddle and whispered fiercely, "Only two more to win it, guys—let's do it!"

7. What can you conclude about Carmelita's character?

   A She is lazy and doesn't care about winning.

   B She is fiercely competitive about winning.

   C She would rather be at home reading a good book.

   D She tries hard but isn't cut out for team sports.

8. How does the author reveal Carmelita's character traits to readers?

   F through dialogue between Carmelita and her teammates

   G by explaining what her teammates think about her

   H by describing Carmelita thoughts, words, and actions

   J by revealing the narrator's thoughts about her

Read part of a product recall notice. Then circle the letter of the answer to each question.

> **Name of Recalled Product:** BestHome 8-cup electric coffee makers
>
> **Manufacturer:** BestHome, Inc., of Morley, Connecticut, www.besthomeinc.com
>
> **Problem:** The glass carafe can shatter, posing cut and burn hazards to consumers.
>
> **Description:** This recall involves BestHome brand 8-cup coffee makers sold in black plastic or brushed chrome. Model numbers being recalled are #1052-A (chrome) and # 1052-B (black). Consumers should immediately stop using the recalled product and return it to any BestHome store for a full refund.

9. Which sentence would act as additional supporting evidence for the main idea of the recall notice?

   A   BestHome produces toaster ovens and blenders.

   B   Consumers may prefer our 12-cup coffee maker.

   C   BestHome brews the best coffee by far.

   D   Contact BestHome about all injuries that are directly related to this product recall.

10. If your coffee maker is part of the recall, you should

   F   return the product to any BestHome store for a full refund.

   G   exchange it for a 12-cup coffee maker.

   H   sell the coffee maker at your next yard sale.

   J   continue to use your coffee maker and hope for the best.

Read part of a glossary. Then circle the letter of the answer to each question.

> **Altimeter**   a device used to find a plane's distance above sea level
>
> **Bathyscaphe**   a navigable, submersible vehicle for exploring the deep ocean
>
> **Chassis**   the frame, wheels, and machinery of an automobile
>
> **Flying Bridge**   a small navigational deck above a ship's pilothouse
>
> **Fuselage**   the structure to which an airplane's wing, tail, and engines attach

11. What is most likely the subject of the book that contains this glossary?

   A   the oceans of the world

   B   modes of transportation

   C   space flight

   D   engine repair

12. Where in the glossary would the word *carburetor* be inserted?

   F   between *Bathyscaphe* and *Chassis*

   G   between *Altimeter* and *Bathyscaphe*

   H   between *Chassis* and *Flying Bridge*

   J   after *Flying Bridge*

Read this excerpt from a food service company's employee handbook. Then circle the letter of the answer to each question.

EMPLOYEE HANDBOOK

Section 12: GROOMING AND APPEARANCE

Your personal appearance has a direct impact on how customers perceive the quality of our services and dining areas. For safety and hygiene reasons, you must follow these guidelines in regard to personal hygiene and grooming.

12.1 Personal Hygiene

Hands are the key to cleanliness in food service. Good personal hygiene is always expected. This includes clean hands, fingernails, teeth, hair, and clothes.

Before starting work, wash your hands and arms thoroughly with soap and water. Wash your hands frequently during each shift (be especially thorough if you are involved directly in the preparation of food). Always wash after using the restroom. Always wash after touching any part of your face, hair, or body and after eating, smoking, working with raw food products, and any other time that your hands may become contaminated. If gloves are worn, they must be changed after eating, touching raw food, etc.

12.2 Nail Polish and Nails

Nail polish can chip or peel off and contaminate food. We suggest that you do not wear nail polish or artificial nails to work. It you do, your hands must always be covered with gloves during your shift.

13. Which sentence could be added to Section 12.1 to act as additional supporting evidence for the main idea?

   A Accidents are caused by not knowing the proper way to perform a task.

   B Employees must wash their hands before putting on a new pair of gloves.

   C If you smoke, please be sure to dispose of cigarette butts in a proper receptacle.

   D Employees must wear appropriate professional attire at all times.

14. Before starting their work shift, employees should

   F be sure to use the restroom.

   G remove their nail polish or artificial nails.

   H put on a new pair of gloves.

   J wash their hands and arms thoroughly.

15. According to the passage, what is the result of chipping or peeling nail polish?

   A Hands need to be washed.

   B Gloves need to be changed.

   C Food becomes contaminated.

   D Artificial nails need to be replaced.

Read the letter of recommendation. Then circle the letter of the answer to each question.

> To Whom It May Concern:
>
> Ivan Chu is an excellent fry cook. He would excel in food service or any job that requires patience, listening skills, and an eye for detail. As shift supervisor at Seaside Café, I had the opportunity to observe him in several jobs. Ivan started delivering orders and then bused tables before deciding he wanted to learn to cook.
>
> He is never late for work, volunteers to cover his coworkers' shifts, and always takes his job seriously. It is rare to find such a young employee who sees beyond the seeming monotony of an entry-level job. Ivan has the work ethic to take it to the next level.
>
> I have recommended to company executives that Ivan be promoted to grill work, but Seaside Café policy extends those jobs only to employees who have taken courses in culinary arts. Unfortunately, Ivan has no such training. With no chance to advance, he is seeking employment elsewhere.
>
> I strongly urge you to hire Ivan Chu. You won't find anyone who takes his job more seriously.
>
> Sincerely,
>
> Elena Santarpio

16. What can you conclude about Ivan's character?

    F   He has unrealistic goals.

    G   He is always dissatisfied.

    H   He is ambitious and hardworking.

    J   He is ambitious but lazy.

17. What did Ivan do in the restaurant immediately before he became a fry cook?

    A   did grill work

    B   delivered orders

    C   took some culinary courses

    D   bused tables

18. What was Ms. Santarpio's purpose for writing this letter?

    F   to tell a funny story about Ivan

    G   to describe Ivan's duties as a fry cook

    H   to explain why Ivan was fired

    J   to persuade someone to hire Ivan

19. Which sentence could be added to the letter to act as additional supporting evidence for the main idea?

    A   Everyone at Seaside Café enjoys working with Ivan.

    B   Ivan has called in sick many times.

    C   Ivan never pitches in to help others.

    D   I do not recommend Ivan for this position.

Circle the letter of the answer to each question.

20. Which two words are antonyms?

    F quick, rapid

    G health, illness

    H heartless, cruel

    J hazardous, dangerous

21. Which word is a synonym of *reply*?

    A ask

    B answer

    C repeat

    D request

22. Which two words are homophones?

    F seller, cellar

    G least, greased

    H struck, strike

    J attend, attuned

23. Which word means "of many cultures"?

    A interracial

    B multicultural

    C uncultured

    D intercultural

24. Which is the correct meaning of *simplify*?

    F something that is simple

    G partly simple

    H the opposite of simple

    J to make or become simple

25. Which word is the plural form of *oasis*?

    A oasis

    B oasises

    C oasiss

    D oases

26. Which two words share the same Latin root?

    F visible, vocation

    G portable, poorly

    H projector, injection

    J protect, reject

27. Which phrase means "the tools belonging to the builder"?

    A the builder's tools

    B the builders tools

    C the builders' tools

    D the builders tools'

28. Which group of words belong to the same word family?

    F relationship, relative, really

    G constructive, reconstruction, deconstruct

    H succeed, second, unsuccessful

    J decimal, deconstruct, decorative

29. Which word means "partly sweet"?

    A semisweet

    B parasweet

    C multisweet

    D intersweet

30. Which word is spelled correctly?

    F fotograph

    G photograff

    H photogragh

    J photograph

31. Which word contains a Latin root meaning "carry"?

    A visor

    B instruction

    C projector

    D portable

32 Which contraction is spelled correctly?

    F was'nt

    G dont

    H couldnt'

    J we're

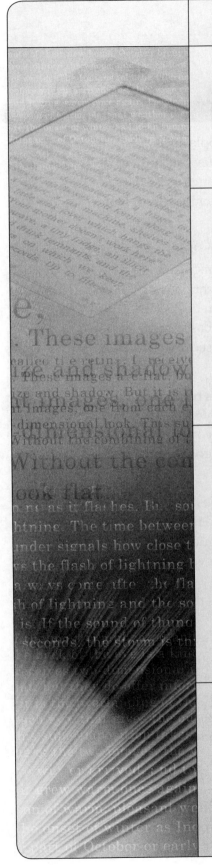

Unit 3

In this unit you will learn how to

You will practice the following workplace skills

You will also learn new words and their meanings and put your reading skills to work in written activities. You will get additional reading practice in *Reading Basics Intermediate 2 Reader*.

Lesson 3.1

Make Generalizations

Writers sometimes make concluding statements that apply to many people, facts, events, or situations. These statements are called generalizations, and they can sum up what has been said or introduce what will be said later. Certain words, such as *most, many, few, all, usually, generally*, and *typically*, can introduce or signal generalizations. Not all generalizations, however, include a signal word.

When you read, it is helpful to be able to both recognize and make generalizations. Making generalizations is similar to drawing conclusions because both require the reader to examine the text and come to a conclusion. Every generalization is a conclusion, but not every conclusion is a generalization. Conclusions can be specific, but when you make a generalization, you come to a general conclusion based on pieces of evidence. Read the example. What generalization could you make based on the examples of specific animals?

> In some cities, it is not unusual to see a deer wander into a person's backyard. Recently, two deer somehow ended up in an empty city lot, happily munching on grass and shrubs. Many people also report hearing the howling of coyotes in the canyons where they live. In one neighborhood, wild turkeys run right across the street on most afternoons.

The passage provides examples about specific animals coming into cities and towns. From this, the reader can make the generalization that wild animals are finding their way to some urban areas. This is a valid generalization: it is based on information in the passage, and it makes sense. Not all generalizations are valid, however. Say that you make this generalization: urban areas are being overrun with wild animals. The information in the passage does not support that generalization, so it is not valid.

Read the passage and decide what valid generalization you can make:

> Everyone on the island attends special events, such as concerts and outdoor movies. In fact, many people volunteer to help at these events. People also take care of the island by never leaving trash on the beach and clearing away seaweed after storms. Most inspiring is the way people take care of each other. Neighbors check on each other and bring meals when someone is sick.

The passage gives specific examples of people on the island helping each other or taking care of the island. A valid generalization you can make is that people on the island take care of their island and of each other.

Read each passage. If the underlined statement is a valid generalization, write *valid*. If it is not a valid generalization, write *not valid*.

Pets make good companions for senior citizens. Some residents of the home where my elderly aunt lives have pets. Being responsible for an animal's care gives people a sense of purpose. These people seem more vibrant and less lonely than the other residents in the home.

1. _____

When writing, use gender-neutral language such as "his or her" to avoid sexism. Of course, when writing about a specific person, you must use gender-specific language. Good writers always use gender-neutral language.

2. _____

During the winter, my skin dries out and cracks. My doctor said that most people have the same problem because the air outside and inside is dry. She recommended using a moisturizing lotion to protect my skin. After I started using it, I learned that my mother and friend also use moisturizer for dry skin. Using moisturizing lotion in winter weather is good for dry skin.

3. _____

I have many friends and neighbors who have pets. When I visit, the dogs usually come to greet me with their tails wagging. They seem happy to see a smiling visitor. On the other hand, the cats usually run and hide under a bed. Dogs are friendlier than cats.

4. _____

Salads is a new fast-food chain that offers fresh, low-calorie meals with no preservatives. It joins Fresh Greens in the healthy fast-food movement. Fast food is always loaded with salt, fat, and chemicals.

5. _____

Read the passages. Write a valid generalization that can be made from information in each passage.

In most books, there are major and minor characters. Minor characters may appear on only a few pages or in only one scene, but they can play a key role in the plot. For example, in the fairy tale *Snow White*, the huntsman is a minor character. However, the rest of the story could not take place if he did not let Snow White escape. Likewise, other minor characters can provide key items or information for the major characters to use.

1. _____

Morphine is sometimes prescribed to relieve pain and relax the nervous system. However, in large amounts it can cause a coma, drowsiness, breathing problems, and eventually death. Copper is a necessary mineral found in the body, but it can cause the liver to fail if taken in large doses. Fluoride hardens tooth enamel and reduces tooth decay when added to toothpaste and drinking water. Taking too much fluoride all at once, however, can be deadly.

2. _____

The Puritans, a religious group, founded Massachusetts. Rhode Island promised religious freedom and separation of church and state. William Penn founded Pennsylvania as a haven for the Quakers and all others who faced religious persecution. Maryland had religious freedom for all.

3. _____

The effects of global warming on our environment are evident. The need to develop renewable energy resources is becoming more urgent than ever. Automobile companies are working to develop cars that run on fuels other than gasoline. Other companies are creating new materials and technologies that generate power from wind, the sun, and heat deep in the ground.

4. _____

Read each passage. Then circle the letter of the answer to each question.

The ancient Greeks used many shapes for coffins, including a triangular coffin that allowed the corpse to be buried in a sitting position. Chaldean coffins were clay urns that were formed around the body, encasing it closely. Some Native Americans buried their dead between the upper and lower shells of a turtle. Others put their dead in canoes that they mounted on scaffolds, or they placed them in wicker baskets that they floated into a stream or lake. Today, in Ghana, some people choose fantasy coffins. These coffins are large replicas of items that represent people's interests.

1. What generalization can you make about coffins based on the evidence in the passage?

   A   Coffins are not always rectangular wooden boxes.

   B   Chaldean coffins were difficult to make.

   C   Native Americans did not have enough wood to make European-style coffins.

   D   Coffins have gotten more serious and formal over the years.

2. What generalization can you make about the way people treat their dead based on the evidence in this passage?

   F   People have not paid much attention to burying their dead.

   G   All Native Americans disposed of their dead in the same way.

   H   The ways people have buried the dead have varied widely among cultures.

   J   Ancient Greeks could not make up their mind about what coffin shape was best.

The American pony express was a mail route that went from Missouri to California. It lasted only 18 months before the telegraph made it obsolete. It wasn't even an original idea. Both Persia and China had horseback mail routes long before the pony express came along in 1860. Marco Polo told of a similar system in China during the 13th century. Pony express riders changed horses at a rest station every 15 miles and generally had a 75-mile workday. Today, the National Parks Service protects many miles of the original mail route. Each year riders take their ponies along the route in honor of the pony express.

3. What generalization can you make about the history of the pony express?

   A   The pony express was never very effective.

   B   It took hundreds of years to perfect the American pony express.

   C   The American pony express was exactly like that of the Chinese.

   D   The idea of a pony express had roots in other cultures of long ago.

Workplace Skill: Make Generalizations in Fact-checking Guidelines

To ensure the accuracy of information in reports, presentations, or workplace documents, you should fact-check certain kinds of information. Use context to figure out the meaning of any unfamiliar words before making a generalization.

Read the guidelines. Then circle the letter of the answer to each question.

Fact-checking Guidelines

Our company guidelines will provide quick and handy information on what to look out for when fact-checking. Please note that the following guidelines must be customized for each project to match the client's particular needs..

Check:

* Quotes

* Dates

* Numbers and Math

* Statistics

* Technical/Factual Information

1. Use tools available to you, including the dictionary, style guide, spell-checker, reference books, and websites.

2. Provide at least two printed pieces of back-up material from a credible source for each fact. For online sources (see list of credible sources below), be sure that the URL and the date that the site was accessed are included on the printout.

3. In the back-up material, underline or highlight relevant information.

Examples of Credible Sources:

The Smithsonian Institution

The White House

The Bureau of Labor Statistics

National Aeronautics and Space Administration (NASA)

---

1. From the guidelines, we can generalize that

   A government websites are usually credible sources.

   B the White House website is a credible source.

   C encyclopedias are usually not credible sources.

   D museum websites are usually not credible sources.

2. What is the meaning of the word *customized* as used in the guidelines?

   F handled

   G increased

   H adjusted

   J removed

Write for Work

You are preparing a report on whether the number of manufacturing jobs in the United States increased or decreased last year. Find three credible sources to gather and fact-check the information in your report. Write the sources in a notebook.

 **Reading Extension**

Turn to "The Mokele-Mbembe: Are All the Dinosaurs Gone?" on page 85 of *Reading Basics Intermediate 2 Reader*. After you have read and/or listened to the article, answer the questions below.

Circle the letter of the answer to each question.

1. Based on the article, what is one generalization you can make about expeditions to find Mokele-Mbembe?

    A They are all successful.

    B Most expeditions have been successful.

    C None of the expeditions has been successful.

    D No one has reported seeing the creature.

2. Based on paragraph 11, what generalization can you make about Mokele-Mbembe?

    F It is definitely a dinosaur.

    G It does not exist.

    H It might be another animal.

    J Nothing lives in that part of the jungle.

3. What generalization can you make about the people who search for Mokele-Mbembe?

    A They will find the creature.

    B They hope to find proof of a living dinosaur.

    C They don't understand extinction.

    D They are unfamiliar with tropical Africa.

Write the answer to each question.

4. Why would remote areas of tropical Africa be the most likely place for a dinosaur to live?

    _____

5. What items did Regusters claim were proof of the beast's existence when he looked for it in 1981?

    _____

Explore Words

BASE WORDS AND ROOTS

Many words in English consist of base words or roots to which prefixes, suffixes, and other endings have been added. A base word can stand alone, while a root cannot. Many roots come from Greek and Latin. For example, in the word *repayment*, *pay* is a base word. In the word *devisable*, *vis* is a Latin root.

Read each group of words. Circle the two words in each group that have the same base word or root.

1. grateful	gratitude	greatly	**4.** portable	vacation	transportation
2. create	cranium	recreation	**5.** market	magnitude	magnificent
3. empty	employ	unemployed	**6.** sanity	sensible	insane

THE SCHWA SOUND

The schwa sound is the sound *uh* that you can hear in the second syllable of the word *postal*. In *postal*, the schwa sound is represented by the letter *a*, but every vowel can stand for the schwa sound. In two-syllable words, the first syllable is usually accented. The schwa sound is heard in the unaccented syllable. For example, say these words: *barrel*, *pencil*, *gallop*, and *channel*. The second syllable in each word is unaccented and contains the schwa sound.

Say the two-syllable words below. Write each syllable on the line and circle the unstressed syllable that contains the schwa sound.

1. broken _____ _____

2. lemon _____ _____

3. idol _____ _____

4. victim _____ _____

5. bacon _____ _____

6. label _____ _____

7. helpful _____ _____

8. rascal _____ _____

9. solid _____ _____

10. human _____ _____

Some words have more than one meaning. For example, a train is a mode of transportation. Used another way, *train* also means "to teach." You can use context clues—other words in the same or nearby sentences—to help you figure out which meaning is intended.

Use context clues in each sentence that help you know the intended meaning of the underlined word. Circle the letter of the intended meaning.

1. Every student seemed <u>engaged</u> by the fascinating guest speaker.
   a. having agreed to get married
   b. interested and involved

2. It is against the law to <u>discriminate</u> because of age.
   a. make a clear distinction
   b. act with prejudice

3. I'm sorry, but your coupon has <u>expired</u>.
   a. ceased to live
   b. is no longer valid

4. Is Baltimore on the <u>coast</u>, or is it inland?
   a. the shore of an ocean
   b. to move without effort

ACADEMIC VOCABULARY

Knowing these high-frequency words will help you in many school subjects.

event	something that happens
typically	characteristic of a particular person or thing
introduce	to occur at the start of
minor	lesser in importance
found	to establish

Complete the sentences below using one of the words above.

1. Afya hopes to _____ a school in her hometown.

2. Camisha hardly gave it a thought. It was a _____ annoyance.

3. That _____ stood out in my memory more than any other.

4. The writer will _____ the characters with short descriptions at the beginning of the story.

5. Diego _____ eats breakfast at 8 A.M. before he goes to the gym at 9 A.M.

Lesson 3.2

Recognize Author's Effect and Intention

An author's intention is what he or she hopes the reader will take away from his or her text. To accomplish this, an author must decide on an approach toward the material and audience.

Style techniques such as word choice, language, and sentence structure create an effect, such as humor, sarcasm, excitement, anger, or suspense. For example, an author may use formal language to create an authoritative effect, or he or she may use casual, informal language to create a friendly effect. Read the example:

> Longing for a cruise of a lifetime? You'll want to try the Ice Queen Cruise Line. It will seem like a lifetime has passed by the time you get off. Short on staff and long on overheated cabins, this ship will take you on an endurance cruise you won't soon forget. As for the food—bring your own or suffer the consequences of the so-called delicacies put before you.

In the passage above, the author's intention is to give a negative review of a cruise line. This author has used style techniques—the choice of sarcastic phrases and the use of direct address—to create an effect of humor and scorn. The effect reveals that the author's intention is to convey the terrible service on the cruise line. If the intention of the author were to give a positive review, he or she would not include sarcastic phrases in the passage but might still employ direct address. The author would also include descriptive details about the positive aspects of the cruise.

Read the passage. Identify the author's effect and intention.

> I would like to take next Wednesday off for my sister's graduation. I do not think this will pose a problem. I am certain that I can complete my assigned portion of the project before Wednesday. In addition, if anything unexpected does arise at the beginning of the week, I can work longer hours. On the day itself, I will check my e-mail periodically and answer any urgent questions. My sister's graduation is very important to my relatives and to me. As the first person in our family to go to college, she is an inspiration to all of us. I know she would be very disappointed were I to miss this momentous event in her life.

From the passage, you can conclude that the author's intention is to convince his or her boss to give him or her the day off. The author uses respectful and serious language to create an effect of importance and formality.

Read each passage. Then circle the letter of the answer to each question.

Kento heard a crash come from the back of the house. He stood and listened carefully but didn't hear anything. He walked down the long, dark, narrow hallway toward his bedroom, thinking the worst. He held his breath as he nudged open the door. Lying face down on the floor was a shattered picture frame that had fallen off the wall. Being a believer of bad omens, Kento wondered whether this omen was meant to warn him of something grim to come.

1. What effect is created by the author's writing style?

   A suspense

   B humor

2. Based on the passage, what do you think the author's intention was for writing?

   F to narrate a story about a man who believes in bad omens

   G to describe how omens can be ominous

The small cat stretched her paws out as far as they would go in opposing directions. The sun streaked down over her, and her white fur seemed to glow. The sequins on her collar sparkled like glitter. As she brought her paw up to her mouth and started grooming herself, she paused, her tiny pink tongue sticking out between her teeth.

3. What effect is created by the author's writing style?

   A suspense

   B peacefulness

4. Based on the passage, what do you think the author's intention was for writing?

   F to describe a scene so that readers can picture it easily

   G to describe how cats groom themselves

Annie Oakley was the sharpest shooter in Buffalo Bill's Wild West show, where she was the show's star for 16 years. In her act, she would shoot a dime out of her husband's hand or a playing card that had been tossed in the air. She once shot a cigarette out of the mouth of the crown prince of Germany at his insistence. She was so good that the Sioux chief Sitting Bull was said to have called her "Little Sure Shot."

5. What effect is created by the author's writing style?

   A uncertainty

   B authority

6. Based on the passage, what do you think the author's intention was for writing?

   F to convey Oakley's skill at shooting

   G to convince readers that Oakley was the sharpest shooter in the Wild West show

Read each passage and answer the questions.

Wasps build nests that are a lot like beehives, but wasps don't make honey—they raise young wasps in their nests. In each part of the nest, the queen wasp lays one egg that will hatch into a kind of larva called a grub. It stays a larva for one to three weeks and then spins a cocoon and becomes a pupa. Inside the cocoon, the pupa changes, developing wings. At last, the adult, winged creature breaks free of its cocoon.

1. What style technique has the author of this passage used?

_____

2. What effect is created by the writing style? Is it authoritative or informal?

_____

3. What do you think the author's intention was for writing?

_____

Decorating cakes does not have to be as challenging as people commonly make it out to be. There are a few basic techniques. Master these and you'll look like a pro in no time. The first and most important step in cake decorating is leveling your cake so you'll have a flat surface to work on. When your cake is level, frosting it will be a breeze. Use a bread knife held horizontally to flatten out each layer, slicing off any excess cake that may have domed up in the center. This is the best part because you get to eat the scraps without anyone knowing.

4. How does the style of this passage contrast with the style of the first passage on the page?

_____

5. What effect is created by the author's approach to the material?

_____

6. Which words and phrases help create this effect?

_____

7. What do you think the author's intention was for writing?

_____

Read each passage. Then circle the letter of the answer to each question.

If you come to dinner with me instead of going to the movies, you'll have a better time on two fronts: entertainment and food. At the restaurant, they will give you a menu filled with items, and you will be able to choose any that you like. At the movies, you'll only have a choice between overpriced popcorn with artificial butter flavoring and candy so old it has dust on the tops of the boxes. Food at the restaurant will probably provide you with at least some nutrients, while popcorn will only give you pieces of kernel that get stuck underneath your gum. You may be saying to yourself, "Yes, but what about the entertainment that the movie will give me?" To this I say, "What could be more entertaining than my sparkling wit?"

1. The effect of the author's language is a feeling of

  A seriousness.   **C** anger.

  B humor.   **D** suspense.

2. From this passage you can conclude that the author's intention is to

  F invite a client to a formal business dinner.

  G describe the new menu of a restaurant.

  H describe how awful going to the movies can be.

  J convince a friend to change his or her plans.

I went to get my flu shot last week, and I really think I should get a medal. I know that getting a flu shot is no big deal. Most people get the shot every year and don't make a fuss. This year, however, a week before I was supposed to get the shot, I kept having the same dream: a 10-foot needle with wings was flying after me. When it was finally my turn to get the real shot, I clenched both fists and clamped my eyes shut. A mere few seconds later it was over, but they were the longest few seconds of my life.

3. The effect of the author's language is a feeling of

  A formality.   **C** fear.

  B anger.   **D** mystery.

4. From this passage you can conclude that the author's intention is to

  F narrate a story about being afraid.

  G convince readers that getting a shot is easy.

  H inspire others to overcome their fears.

  J describe why it is important to get a flu shot.

Workplace Skill:
Recognize Author's Effect and Intention in a Workplace Poster

Companies can communicate with their employees in many ways—e-mails, company meetings, employee handbooks, even a poster. Posters are usually placed in key locations within the company so all employees can see and read them.

Read the poster. Then circle the letter of the answer to each question below the box.

Get a Flu Shot This Fall!

*Did you know?—Flu is caused by the influenza virus, which can be spread by coughing, sneezing, or nasal secretions. By getting vaccinated, you can protect yourself from influenza and may also avoid spreading influenza to others. It takes up to two weeks for protection to develop after the shot. Protection lasts about one year.

*Did you know?—An infected person can spread the influenza virus 24 hours before the onset of his or her illness and up to three to five days after. This makes the typical factory environment the perfect breeding ground for the flu. This year's vaccine will protect against three strains of influenza, including H1N1, so there is only one flu shot this year!

*Our company—Management believes that good health care can be convenient, affordable, and accessible to all. Please join us this year to help yourself and your coworkers, friends, and family avoid an unnecessary illness.

Experienced Nursing Staff	Simple and Convenient
All immunizations are administered by licensed nurses with extensive medical experience, never by a medical technician or pharmacist.	Receive a shot without leaving the building or scheduling an appointment. You may either preregister online or register in person on the day of the event.

FLU SHOT SCHEDULE	
Tuesday, October 19, 8:00 A.M. – 12:30 P.M.	Tuesday, November 2, 2:00 – 5:00 P.M.

The cost is $25.00 per flu vaccination.

1. The author's intention in writing this poster is to

  A scare employees about a possible flu epidemic.

  B encourage employees to have a flu shot in order to keep flu outbreaks to a minimum.

  C encourage employees to think about the drawbacks of the flu virus.

  D change company policy to include extra sick days.

2. The effect of the author's language is a feeling of

  F anger.

  G fear.

  H encouragement.

  J disappointment.

Write for Work

Your company is starting an employee exercise program, and you have been recruited to design and write a poster. Think about your intention in writing the poster and why an exercise program could be beneficial. Think about the effect you want your poster to have on employees. In a notebook, write one sentence about your intention and one sentence about its effect.

  Reading Extension

Turn to "Spiritualism: Fact or Fraud" on page 93 of *Reading Basics Intermediate 2 Reader*. After you have read and/or listened to the article, answer the questions below.

Circle the letter of the answer to each question.

1. Read paragraph 13. What do you think the author's intention was for including the detail about Mary Todd Lincoln?

   A   to show that Mary Todd Lincoln was crazy

   B   to show that Mary Todd Lincoln was easily fooled

   C   to show that even the famous and wealthy can be swindled

   D   to show how famous the Fox sisters had become

2. What do you think the author's intention was in writing this article?

   F   to show that spiritualism is a hoax

   G   to show that spiritualism is valid

   H   to present spiritualism in a neutral way

   J   to show that the Fox sisters were telling the truth but that Leonora Piper was a liar

Write the answer to each question.

3. Read paragraph 18. What do you think the author's intention was for including this information?

   _____

   _____

4. What effect is created by the description of Leonora's second visit to the psychic in paragraph 20?

   _____

   _____

Explore Words

PREFIXES

A prefix is a word part that can be added to the beginning of many base words or roots. Adding prefixes to base words and roots changes their meaning. The prefixes *in-*, *im-*, *il-*, and *ir-* all mean "not." For example, the word *infrequent* means "not frequent," and the word *irresponsible* means "not responsible."

Read the passage. Then circle the nine words that have the prefix *in-*, *im-*, *il-*, or *ir-*.

Many people think it's improper to have tattoos, even if clothing makes them invisible. I was impatient to get a tattoo, but at the time it was illegal where I live. So I traveled to another state, even though it was inconvenient. Some friends thought I was irrational to get one. Some of the things they said were inaccurate and very impolite! I don't think my decision was irresponsible. In fact, it was the right decision for me, and I don't regret it.

SUFFIXES *-ion*, *-tion*

A suffix is a word part that can be added to the end of a word to change its meaning. The suffixes *-ion* and *-tion* mean "the act, quality, or state of." The word *depression* is made up of *depress* and *-ion*. It means "the state of being depressed."

destruction	attention	celebration	exceptions
explanation	reflection	collision	illustrations

Read the sentences. Write a word from the box above to complete each sentence.

1. Come to my family's _____ when Sam graduates from high school.

2. My car needed a new fender after the _____.

3. It's hard to pay _____ when you haven't had enough sleep.

4. The _____ in this book were done with watercolors.

5. Can you see your _____ in the water?

6. There are always _____ to the rules.

7. The earthquake in Haiti caused a great deal of _____.

8. Do you have a good _____ for being late?

SPELLING: PLURALS OF NOUNS ENDING IN -o

Plural nouns are nouns that name more than one person, place, or thing.

- To form the plural of words that end with a vowel and *o*, add *-s (radio/radios)*.
- To form the plural of words that end with a consonant and *o*, add *-s (piano/pianos)* or *-es (potato/potatoes)*. Check the dictionary for the correct spelling.

Write the plural form of each word on the line. Use a dictionary if you're not sure.

1. patio _____

2. tomato _____

3. echo _____

4. memo _____

5. hero _____

6. studio _____

7. rodeo _____

8. stereo _____

ACADEMIC VOCABULARY

Knowing these high-frequency words will help you in many school subjects.

intention a goal or plan

approach a way of dealing with something

technique a way of doing something

assign to designate a job or duty

common seen often

Complete the sentences below using one of the words above.

1. The runner had no _____ of quitting the race even though he started to feel sick.

2. Alma thought her manager would _____ her the task of organizing the files because she had done such a good job of it last year.

3. Nuri's first attempt didn't work out, so he changed his _____ to the problem.

4. Georgia O'Keefe's paintings show a mastery of the watercolor _____.

5. It is _____ to see people eating lunch on the benches by the fountain.

Lesson 3.3

Compare and Contrast

INTRODUCE

When you think about how two or more things are alike, you are making comparisons. For example, you might compare how coffee and tea are alike by describing how they both usually have caffeine and are served hot. When you contrast two or more things, you think about how they are different. You might contrast how coffee and tea are different by describing how coffee is brewed from ground beans while tea is brewed from leaves.

Writers may use a pattern of comparison and contrast to give their writing more interest. When writing has been organized to show comparison and contrast, readers can visualize what they are reading about and can recognize how ideas are related.

Oftentimes, writers use certain clue words to let readers know when they are comparing or contrasting. Read these sample clue words and phrases.

Words or Phrases that Compare
alike, by comparison, similar to, both, likewise, also

Words or Phrases that Contrast
different, but, while, however, although, unlike, on the other hand

To compare and contrast, ask yourself: How are these two topics alike, and how are they different? How are the topics related? Read the following passage in which the author compares the ways in which several insects make sounds:

> Some insects have a way of producing sound without using vocal chords. Beetles make noise by rubbing one part of the body against another. Similarly, certain grasshoppers rub a hind leg against a vein in the forewing to "sing."

In the passage above, the word *similarly* indicates comparison. It compares the ways two different kinds of insects make noise.

Read the passage. Note what is being compared and contrasted.

> Onions are grown all over the world, and it sometimes seems like every country has its own distinct size, color, and flavor of onion. Italian onions, which are often used for a garnish because of their red outer rings, are eaten raw. The large onions grown in Spain also taste mild enough to be eaten raw. Bermuda onions are similarly large and mild; however, they have a yellow or white color.

Did you note that the properties of onions are being compared and contrasted? The colors and flavors of onions in different countries are compared and contrasted.

Read each passage. Then answer the questions.

Many people have heard of killer bees but have not heard of killer ants. Fire ants are a type of ant that can hurt or kill people. Like killer bees, they are aggressive insects that swarm and attack when disturbed. Just like the stings of killer bees, the stings of fire ants can make people ill or even cause them to die in rare cases. Both killer bees and red imported fire ants came to North America from other places.

1. What two things are being compared? _____

2. Name two ways in which they are alike. _____

_____

Some elements are hard and dull solids, some are colorless and odorless gases, and some are liquids. Metals conduct heat and electricity well, are bendable, and can be polished to a shine. Nonmetals are poor conductors, are brittle and dull, and usually exist as solids or gases at room temperature. Metalloids have properties of both metals and nonmetals.

3. What things are being compared and contrasted? _____

4. Name two ways in which metals and nonmetals are different. _____

_____

World War I was fought from 1914 to 1918, and World War II lasted from 1939 to 1945. Both were international conflicts, but there were major differences. While 16 countries were directly involved in World War I, World War II involved 27. World War I lasted a little over four years, but World War II lasted almost exactly six years. The cost of World War I—about $200 billion—is dwarfed by the $2 trillion spent on World War II.

5. What two things are being compared and contrasted? _____

6. Write one way in which they are alike and one way in which they are different.

Alike: _____

Different: _____

Read the passage. Then fill in the Venn diagram.

Both international affairs and domestic affairs have political, economic, and social aspects. International affairs involve other countries, but domestic affairs, on the other hand, involve only the United States. Both are important in any presidential administration. International affairs include foreign aid, wars, and trade relationships. Domestic affairs include health-care reform and tax cuts. Both are the subject of laws passed by Congress. International affairs are dealt with mainly at the national level, while domestic affairs affect national, state, and local levels of government.

International Affairs   Both   Domestic Affairs

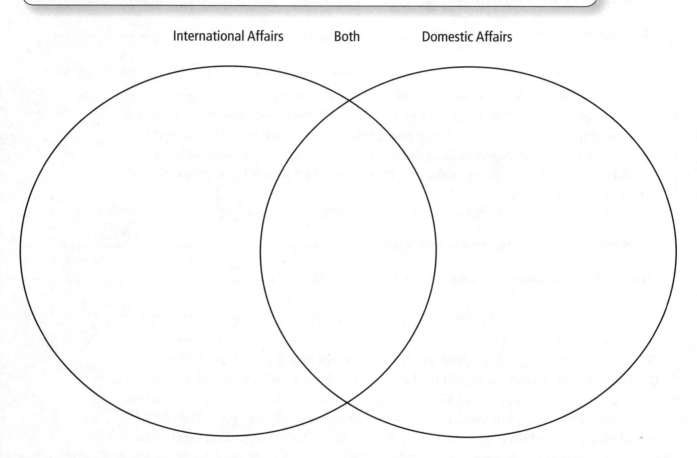

Write the clue words from the passage that helped you fill in the diagram.

_____

_____

Read each passage. Then circle the letter of the answer to each question.

Different kinds of exercises help the body in different ways. Some exercises, such as yoga, produce increased flexibility and range of motion. This helps strengthen ligaments and reduces strain on the joints. Other exercises, such as weight lifting, build stronger muscle. Aerobic exercises, such as bicycling or swimming, help large muscle groups all over the body. This type of exercise also strengthens the heart and lungs.

1. What things are contrasted?

   A ways to reduce joint stress

   B types of exercise equipment

   C ways to strengthen the lungs

   D types of exercise

2. Which is a signal word or phrase that the author uses to show contrast?

   F also

   G in addition

   H different

   J such as

The National League and the American League are the two leagues in modern American professional baseball. Their regular seasons begin and end at the same time. Both leagues have teams all over the country, and both play in the World Series. The National League has 16 teams, while the American League has only 14. One major difference—perhaps the biggest—between the two leagues is the designated hitter rule. Each National League team's roster has nine players, and all players both bat and field. An American League team's roster has 10 players, and the extra player is the designated hitter. This player doesn't have a fielding position, but he takes the pitcher's place in the batting lineup.

3. What is one thing the National League and the American League have in common?

   A Both play in the World Series.

   B They have the same number of teams.

   C They have the same number of players on the roster.

   D Both have a designated hitter.

4. What is one way in which the National League and the American League are different?

   F The American League has teams in the western United States, while the National League only has teams in the east.

   G All players in the National League bat and field, while in the American League, the pitcher does not bat.

   H They have different season lengths.

   J Only the American League plays in the World Series.

Workplace Skill:
Compare and Contrast with a Graph

Graphs are an easy way to read and understand data. Companies use graphs to more easily follow industry trends. With graphs, you can easily explain your information while still getting your point across clearly and quickly.

Read the graph. Then circle the letter of the answer to each question below the box.

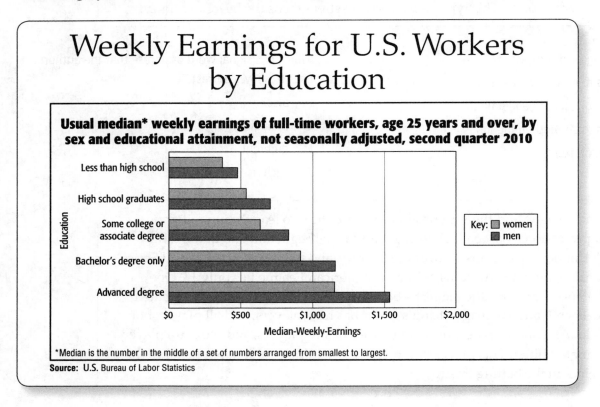

1. If you are a woman with a bachelor's degree, how would your weekly earnings compare to a man with a high school diploma?

   A Your weekly earnings would be the same as the man.

   B Your weekly earnings would be less than the man.

   C You would earn twice as much per week as the man.

   D Your weekly earnings would be higher than the man.

2. In what area of educational attainment were women's weekly earnings most different from men's weekly earnings?

   F Less than high school

   G High school graduates

   H Some college or associate's degree

   J Advanced degree

Write for Work

Suppose you are a career counselor at the local community college. Based on the information in the graph on page 154, how would you advise a student on the benefits of attaining a bachelor's degree versus an associate's degree? In a notebook, explain your reasons.

 Reading Extension

Turn to "Chupacabra: Bloodthirsty Beast" on page 103 of *Reading Basics Intermediate 2 Reader*. After you have read and/or listened to the article, answer the questions below.

Circle the letter of the answer to each question.

1. What mythical creature does the author compare to the Chupacabra?

   A unicorn

   B werewolf

   C dragon

   D vampire

2. What real creature does the author compare to the Chupacabra?

   F cow

   G bat

   H wolf

   J sheep

3. What is one way in which New York City, Moscow, and Naucalpan are alike?

   A They are all in North America.

   B They are all major cities.

   C They have all experienced chupacabra sightings.

   D They have all had confirmed chupacabra attacks.

Write the answer to each question.

4. In paragraph 5, what explanations are given for where the Chupacabra originated?

   _____

   _____

5. In paragraph 9, to what does the farmer compare the Chupacabra?

   _____

   _____

Explore Words

Many English words have Latin roots. When you know the meaning of roots and the meanings of prefixes and suffixes, you can figure out the meanings of unfamiliar words. Look at these common Latin roots, what they mean, and examples of English words that are based on them:

port	"carry"	+	*-able*	"able to be"	*portable* (able to be carried)
tain	"hold"	+	*re-*	"back"	*retain* (hold back)
tract	"pull"	+	*ex-*	"out"	*extract* (pull out)

Write one word that has the Latin root *port*, one word that has the Latin root *tain*, and one word that has the Latin root *tract*. Then find each word in a dictionary and write a short definition.

1. _____ Dictionary definition: _____

2. _____ Dictionary definition: _____

3. _____ Dictionary definition: _____

SUFFIXES *-ous*, *-ious*

A suffix is a word part that can be added to the end of many words. Adding a suffix changes the meaning of a base word or root. For example, the suffixes *-ous* and *-ious* mean "having the quality of." So, the word *furious* means "having the quality of fury" and *glorious* means "having the quality of glory." Notice that the spelling of the base word or root may change when adding the suffixes *-ous* and *-ious*.

Read each phrase and write a word with a suffix that means the same thing as the phrase. Then write a sentence that includes the word.

1. having the quality of adventure _____

_____

2. having the quality of caution _____

_____

3. having the quality of envy _____

_____

A prefix is a word part that can be added to the beginning of a word. Adding a prefix can change the meaning of base words and roots. Some prefixes indicate number. The prefix *uni-* means "one," *bi-* means "two," and *tri-* means "three."

Write the prefix *uni-, bi-,* or *tri-* on the line to make a word with the meaning given.

1. A _____cycle is "a type of cycle with three wheels."

2. A _____logy is "a set of three books."

3. A _____athlon is "an athletic competition consisting of two events."

4. _____annual means "happening twice a year"

5. A _____form is "a single outfit of clothes worn by many people."

6. _____lateral means "relating to the two sides of the body."

7. A _____cuspid is "a tooth characterized by two points."

8. A _____cycle is "a type of cycle with one wheel."

9. _____angle means "a shape with three sides and three angles."

10. _____cultural means "coming from two cultures."

11. _____coastal means "relating to both the east and west coasts of the United States."

12. _____color means "having three colors."

ACADEMIC VOCABULARY

Knowing these high-frequency words will help you in many school subjects.

compare to show how things are alike

contrast a difference; to show how things are different

relate to be connected

distinct easily and unmistakably recognized

property quality or trait

Complete the sentences below using one of the words above.

1. Eduardo admired the speaker because he could _____ to his story.

2. It is difficult to _____ the two women because they are so different.

3. One attractive _____ of the stone was its shiny surface.

4. The _____ between the before and after make-over pictures was amazing.

5. The class separated into two _____ groups.

Lesson 3.4

Predict Outcomes

Predicting an outcome means making a logical guess about what will happen next based on the information you have. Predicting keeps you involved in a story or article, and it can add interest to your reading. When you predict, use clues in the text along with your prior knowledge and experience to make guesses that are reasonable, or that make sense, about what will happen next in a passage.

Suppose you read about a person putting on a bathing suit, smearing on sunscreen, and then picking up a towel. A prediction would be that the next thing the person will do is go swimming outside in a sunny location.

When predicting outcomes, look for these kinds of clues:

- suggestions of what will happen next in a sequence of events
- statements of causes and possible effects
- suggestions of how a person will behave in a given situation or has behaved before in a similar situation

Then think about times when you may have experienced something similar to what you are reading and what the outcome of that was. Use this information together with the textual clues to make predictions.

Remember to adjust your prediction as you read. New information may be revealed that changes your prediction. Predictions should make sense with what you have read up to that point, but they may not always turn out to be correct.

Read the passage. Use context clues and what you already know to predict what might happen next.

Winona was eager to submit an application for a promotion to her boss. The deadline was the next day at 10 A.M. She was just revising her short statement when her friend Emelia called with tickets to the local minor-league baseball team's play-off game that evening. Winona is not much of a baseball fan.

Do you predict that Winona will not go to the game so she can finish her application? The clues are that she is eager to apply for a promotion and that she is not much of a baseball fan. Because she is not a fan, tickets to a minor-league game—even a play-off game—will probably not interest her enough to give up work on her application.

Read each passage. Then predict the outcome. Write what you think will happen next.

Many tales and legends have been told and written about the sly and clever fox. One of these, called "The Fox and the Fleas," tells about a fox with a flea problem. Hoping to rid himself of fleas, the fox decides to submerge himself in water and drown the fleas. He slowly sinks beneath the surface of a lake, holding a piece of wool in his mouth that floats above the water line. As the water laps over him, the fleas abandon their place in his fur and make their way onto the wool, the only dry spot around. What will the fox do next?

1. _____

Kailani is a talented singer who wants to go to music school and study opera. She has worked hard all her life to be the best in everything she does, and she usually gets praised for her work. Her teacher says that she will not be accepted to a music school because her audition songs all sound the same. What will Kailani do next?

2. _____

Effective advertisements can help volunteer and charity organizations garner support from the public. During the First and Second World Wars, the American Red Cross created a "knit your bit" campaign that encouraged volunteers to knit warm clothes for refugees and soldiers. The Red Cross provided patterns for items that went with military clothing. The Red Cross also instructed volunteers to use certain colors to match military uniforms. What do you think people did?

3. _____

_____

Sanura loves cheese more than any other food. She's written articles on the use of cheese in food for the local paper. She reads books and magazines about different types of cheese and where they can be found. She sees an ad for a job as a cheese monger at the upscale market in town. What will she do next?

4. _____

_____

Read each situation. Then circle the letter of the outcome you think would be most likely, and explain why you chose that outcome.

An experienced mountain climber has dreamed of climbing a certain peak for over a decade. He has been planning this climb for a long time. He sets out one morning, but before he gets far in his climb, he sees heavy storm clouds coming his way.

1. **A** The climber reaches the top.

   B The climber dies in the storm.

   C The climber turns back.

   D The climber decides never to climb again.

2. _____

One seemingly nice spring day, a family with five children planned an outing. They planned to hike in the nearby woods and then eat a picnic lunch. They did not check the weather report before they left even though it had been a very wet month.

3. **F** The family had a wonderful day.

   G It started to rain, and they went home.

   H Someone got lost.

   J They met another family and joined them for their picnic.

4. _____

Irina works for weeks on a big presentation at work, and she is extremely nervous even though she's made dozens of similar presentations. She researches the potential client and studies business trends in related fields for the last 10 years. On the day of the presentation, she breaks a heel on her shoe, gets a paper cut, and forgets to eat lunch. At last, the client and her team assemble for her presentation.

5. **A** Irina overcomes her obstacles, and the presentation is a success.

   B The presentation is a failure because Irina is flustered from her morning.

   C Irina becomes too upset to give the presentation.

   D Irina asks another colleague to give the presentation even though he doesn't know anything about it.

6. _____

Read each situation. Then circle the letter of the answer that predicts the most logical outcome.

A famous nature photographer was taking pictures in the rain forest near a precarious slope. Trying to get a better view of a pair of monkeys in a tree, she stretched out, balancing on her left leg while reaching up the slope with her right. Suddenly, she began to slip on the damp earth and wet leaves. Luckily, as she began to slide backward, she was able to reach out with a free hand.

1. What will happen next?

A She will slide down the slope and then climb back up to take the picture.

B She will steady herself and take the picture.

C She will throw her camera down and use both hands to protect herself.

D She will use her camera strap to lasso a branch.

For most of her life, Linh has been interested in ancient Egypt. She has read all she can about the culture and history of ancient Egypt and has seen movies and documentaries about the country. She has learned Arabic and has visited many different museums with Egyptian collections. When her aunt dies, Linh inherits $5,000.

2. What will Linh do next?

F She will bid on a sarcophagus.

G She will make a documentary about Egypt.

H She will upgrade her apartment.

J She will take a trip to Egypt.

While exploring a cave with their professor, a group of students make some incredible discoveries. The walls of a back cavern of the cave have very ancient-looking drawings of animals on them. The students also discover fossilized human remains and primitive-looking tools.

3. What will happen next?

A The group will keep the discovery a secret.

B The students will bury the bones.

C The group will contact the archeology department at their school.

D The students will sell the bones to a museum.

Workplace Skill: Predict Outcomes Using an Organizational Flowchart

Organizational flowcharts are easy-to-understand diagrams that note everyone's area of responsibility at an organization and to whom they report. They present a clear picture of how a company or department is organized. Organizational flowcharts can be used by both employees and job applicants to make predictions about where to direct a particular question or issue in order to efficiently produce a desired outcome.

Read the organizational flowchart. Then circle the letter of the answer to each question below the box.

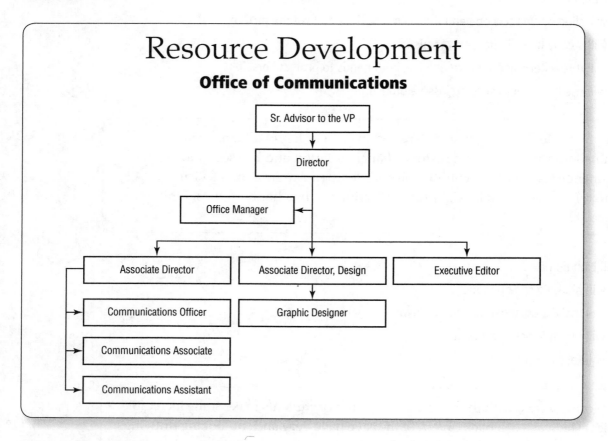

1. The Associate Director, Design is having a problem meeting a deadline for the design of a company brochure. He needs to communicate this to the person to whom he reports. He will report first to the

   A Communications Officer.

   B Associate Director.

   C Director.

   D Communications Associate.

2. The Director needs to request a meeting with the head of her department. She will send her e-mail to the

   F Associate Director.

   G Executive Editor.

   H Graphic Designer.

   J Sr. Advisor to the Vice President.

Write for Work

In your own words in a notebook, explain why an organizational flowchart can be useful both to an employee of a company and to a job applicant.

 Reading Extension

Turn to "Challenger: The Final Countdown" on page 111 of *Reading Basics Intermediate 2 Reader*. After you have read and/or listened to the article, answer the questions below.

Circle the letter of the answer to each question.

1. On page 111, which does NOT provide a clue to help the reader prepare for what happens later?

   A the title of the article

   B the lesson number

   C the photograph

   D the caption

2. In paragraph 2, what details about McAuliffe's childhood would allow the reader to predict that she would apply to be the first teacher in space?

   F She was always envious of astronauts.

   G She was among 11,000 teachers who submitted applications.

   H She was a social studies teacher.

   J She lived in New Hampshire.

3. What clue is given in paragraph 6 to let the reader know what might happen?

   A Students and faculty were cheering loudly.

   B It was unusually cold.

   C People were chanting in unison.

   D The families of the Challenger crew were on the roof.

Write the answer to each question.

4. Was there any reason for people watching on television to think that there would be a problem with the launch? Explain your answer.

   _____

5. Paragraph 14 states that it was two and a half years before another U.S. shuttle was launched. Can you predict any other effects this event might have had on the space program?

   _____

Explore Words

A suffix is a word part that can be added to the end of many words. Adding suffixes to base words and roots changes their meanings. Look at these suffixes, their meanings, words that include them, and what the words mean.

myth	"traditional story"	+	*-ic*	"pertaining to"	*mythic* (pertaining to myth)
refuse	"decline"	+	*-al*	"the act of"	*refusal* (act of refusing)
nice	"good"	+	*-ly*	"in such a way"	*nicely* (in a nice way)

Some words have more than one suffix. For example, look at the word *mythically*. It includes the suffixes *-ic*, *-al*, and *-ly*, which have been added to the base word *myth*.

Read each word. Then write the base word and the suffixes or word endings on the lines. The first item has been done for you.

1. methodical   *method*   *ic*   *al*

2. historical   _____   _____   _____

3. biographical   _____   _____   _____

4. quickly   _____   _____   _____

5. economical   _____   _____   _____

6. rhythmic   _____   _____   _____

7. smoothly   _____   _____   _____

A prefix is a word part that can be added to the beginning of many words. Adding prefixes to base words and roots changes their meanings. The prefixes *en-* and *em-* mean "to put in" or "to make or cause." For example, the word *entomb* means "to put in a tomb," and *enrich* means "to make rich."

Draw a line from each word in the second column to its meaning in the first column.

1. to put in a cage   **a.** enrage

2. to make dear   **b.** entangle

3. to cause rage   **c.** endear

4. to make tangled   **d.** embattle

5. to put into battle   **e.** encage

As you read, you may come across unfamiliar words. You can use context clues to help you figure out what these unfamiliar words mean. Context clues are other words in the same sentence or in nearby sentences that help you understand the meaning of the unknown word.

Write the meaning of each underlined word on the line.

1. Few things are more <u>functional</u> than a paper bag. It is useful in so many ways.

Functional means _____.

2. Shoulder pads make women's shoulders look bigger, but they <u>minimize</u> the look of their waists.

Minimize means _____.

3. The book of riddles was <u>inane</u>, but I enjoyed it because sometimes I like foolish things.

Inane means _____.

4. As José described her, an <u>image</u> of his daughter came into my mind. I could picture exactly how she looked.

An *image* is a _____.

ACADEMIC VOCABULARY

Knowing these high-frequency words will help you in many school subjects.

predict	to make a guess about something that will happen based on clues
outcome	result
logical	clearly and soundly reasoned
prior	previous
adjust	to change

Complete the sentences below using one of the words above.

1. The race was so close that no one could _____ the winner.

2. After the accident, the next _____ step was to call the insurance company.

3. Neva had to _____ her thinking after she read the groundbreaking study.

4. The _____ of the shopping expedition was new shoes.

5. Jaha couldn't accept the invitation because she had a _____ commitment.

Lesson 3.5

Identify Fact and Opinion

To understand what you read and hear, you need to be able to distinguish facts from opinions. A fact is a statement that can be verified, or proven. A fact could be a location, a historic event, a statistic, a specific date, or other information that can be objectively tested and proven. An opinion gives a person's belief or viewpoint about something. Some opinions are directly stated, while others are implied by speech or actions. Some types of writing, such as editorials, use a combination of facts and opinions to show the writer's view. Words such as *should, believe, think, everyone,* and *no one* often signal opinions.

To determine if something is a fact or an opinion, ask yourself if you can prove it by looking it up or testing it. Read the examples below.

Fact: Eleanor Roosevelt was the wife of President Franklin Delano Roosevelt.

Opinion: Mrs. Roosevelt was a more interesting individual than her husband.

Remember that a belief or viewpoint is still an opinion even if many or most people agree with the statement. Another thing to note is that incorrect facts are still facts. Incorrect facts can be disproved. For example:

Fact: Franklin Delano Roosevelt was elected four times to the presidency.

False Fact: Franklin Delano Roosevelt was elected five times to the presidency.

Read the passage. Underline the statements that are facts and circle the statements that are opinions.

(1) Faults in Earth's surface can run through land as well as beneath the oceans. (2) Undersea faults have the potential to create destructive ocean waves. (3) Some people call these *tidal waves.* (4) No one should use this term, however. (5) The waves that form from faults on the ocean floor have nothing to do with ocean tides. (6) Scientists use the Japanese word *tsunami,* meaning "harbor wave," as a more precise term for the destructive waves created by the movement of undersea faults.

You should have underlined every sentence except sentence 4. The statements in sentences 1, 2, 3, 5, and 6 are facts. They can be proved by looking up the information in an encyclopedia or other reliable reference source. Sentence 4 states an opinion, which cannot be proven. The words *no one* and *should* in the fourth sentence signal to the reader that these are opinions.

Read the statements. Decide whether each statement is a fact or an opinion. Write each statement in the appropriate column in the graphic organizer.

Marian Anderson was a famous African American singer.

Anderson was the first African American soloist to sing with the New York City Metropolitan Opera.

Marian Anderson was the best opera singer in America.

Arturo Toscanini was a conductor who said that a voice like Anderson's "comes once in 100 years."

In 1939 Anderson was barred from performing in Constitution Hall because she was African American.

She gave a concert in front of the Lincoln Memorial in Washington, D.C., instead.

More than 75,000 people came out that day to see Anderson perform.

It is shameful that racism affected Anderson and her singing career.

Fact	Opinion

Write *F* beside each fact and *O* beside each opinion. Then, for each fact, write the name of one source in which you could find information to prove it. Choose among these sources: encyclopedia, atlas, or newspaper.

_____ **1.** Gwendolyn Brooks, an African American poet, grew up on the South Side of Chicago.

_____

_____ **2.** The Florida panther is a stunning and critically endangered mammal that we must find ways to save.

_____

_____ **3.** Perhaps the world's most beautiful example of a coral reef is the Great Barrier Reef in Australia.

_____

_____ **4.** Australia is the only one of the world's countries that is also a continent.

_____

_____ **5.** It is unfortunate that most Westerners are unfamiliar with traditional Chinese medicine.

_____

_____ **6.** The temperature today will be 75 degrees with a chance of thunderstorms.

_____

_____ **7.** More than 40,000 American troops died at the Battle of Gettysburg during the American Civil War.

_____

_____ **8.** At Utopia Theater, the movie times for today are 12:10 P.M., 3:55 P.M., and 6:20 P.M. only.

_____

_____ **9.** You're better off eating at home before the movie than paying high prices for popcorn.

_____

Circle the letter of the answer to each question.

1. Which of the following is an opinion?

    A Polar bears can be more than five feet tall and weigh as much as 1,600 pounds.

    B An adult polar bear fears no other animal.

    C Polar bears have white fur that covers black skin.

    D The polar bear can rightly be called the king of the North.

2. Which of the following is a fact?

    F People can watch movies at home on television or on DVD.

    G People who talk in movie theaters are very rude.

    H People who want to talk during the movies should stay home.

    J Movie tickets cost way too much these days.

3. Which of the following is an opinion?

    A Everyone should live in New York City at some point in their lives.

    B New York City is nicknamed "The Big Apple."

    C More than 8 million people live in New York City.

    D New York City is made up of five boroughs, of which Brooklyn is the most populous.

4. Which of the following is an opinion?

    F More than 85 colleges and universities are located in Massachusetts.

    G The students at the Massachusetts Institute of Technology are smarter than those at Harvard.

    H Four U.S. presidents were born in Massachusetts.

    J Basketball was invented in Springfield, Massachusetts, in 1891.

5. Which of the following is a fact?

    A James Cameron wrote and directed the movies *Titanic* and *Avatar*.

    B The animation in *Avatar* was amazing.

    C If you didn't see *Avatar* in 3-D, you missed the total experience.

    D *Titanic* was good, but *Avatar* was artistically superior.

6. Which of the following is an opinion?

    F Spain is one of the largest countries in Europe.

    G Spain and Portugal make up the land area known as the Iberian Peninsula.

    H Some regions of Spain have two official languages—Spanish and Catalan.

    J The castles of Spain are the most interesting of all the European castles.

Workplace Skill: Identify Fact and Opinion in a Press Release

A press release is a public relations announcement issued to the news media and other targeted outlets. A company issues press releases to inform the public of company developments. A press release is an attempt to draw media attention to a specific event or product launch. The intention is to publicize a company or a product in the most positive and constructive manner.

Read the press release. Then circle the letter of the answer to each question below the box.

Pacific Food Distributors Offers New Seafood Product Line

FOR IMMEDIATE RELEASE

Sacramento, California, January 22—Pacific Food Distributors is a product specialist for restaurants, retailers, and other food providers. It is pleased to be offering a new, exciting, and delicious seafood product to its customers under the Nautilus brand name. These products come in a variety of sizes to satisfy the needs of restaurant owners and retailers. If you are looking to add a high-quality line of seafood products to your menu, this is the product for you.

(1) Huy Phan, Director of Marketing for Pacific, said, "Our customers have told us that consistency of sizing and quality is essential. (2) We are now able to provide this to our customers in a new product line. (3) Every seafood product that bears the Nautilus name has gone through strict testing. (4) This is a great new product with the best quality on the West Coast.

The Nautilus brand was developed not only to offer quality seafood products to seafood lovers. It also aims to help foster a greater awareness of the sustainability issues that affect our oceans. Phan continued, "The Nautilus brand guarantees that your customers will rave about the superior taste and freshness of our products. They will also appreciate our commitment to ensuring a sustained and productive environment."

For more information please contact:

Belia Sanchez in the Marketing Department of Pacific Food Distributors at 686.258.7838

---

1. Which states an opinion?

  A "these products come in a variety of sizes to satisfy the needs"

  B "a new, exciting, and delicious seafood product"

  C "is a product specialist for restaurants, retailers, and other food providers"

  D "under the Nautilus brand name"

2. Which sentence in paragraph 2 of the press release states an opinion?

  F sentence 1

  G sentence 2

  H sentence 3

  J sentence 4

Write for Work

You are the marketing manager at Arco Pet Supplies. Your company has developed a new treat for dogs. It claims to taste great and also be nutritional for dogs. Your assignment is to write a press release to launch the new product. In a notebook, write a press release using the press release on page 170 as a guide. Your press release should include both facts and opinions.

 Reading Extension

Turn to "Oil, Oil Everywhere" on page 120 of *Reading Basics Intermediate 2 Reader*. After you have read and/or listened to the article, answer the questions below.

Circle the letter of the answer to each question.

1. Which of the following statements is a fact?
   A Third mate Cousins was probably not qualified to steer the *Valdez* through the sound.
   B The Coast Guard should have tracked the ship by radar.
   C Exxon fired Captain Hazelwood after receiving the results from his blood-alcohol test.
   D Exxon should not have ignored Hazelwood's drinking problem.

2. Which of the following statements is an opinion?
   F Exxon spent billions of dollars to clean up Prince William Sound.
   G Hazelwood felt the jolt when the *Valdez* impaled itself on Bligh Reef.
   H Animal rescue centers were being flooded with sick, oily animals.
   J The Valdez crew shouldn't have been short-staffed and fatigued.

3. Which of the following statements is an opinion?
   A Alaska's Prince William Sound is a dazzling jewel in America's last frontier.
   B The jagged coast is dotted with coves and inlets where fish spawn and otters and seals play.
   C Along the shoreline, brown bears catch fish, and deer forage for sea kelp.
   D For years the wildlife and marine life had the sound to themselves.

Write the answer to each question.

4. What is one fact you learned from the article about the Exxon *Valdez*?

_____

5. In your opinion, who or what caused the oil spill? Give reasons.

_____

Explore Words

BASE WORDS AND ROOTS

Many words in English consist of base words or roots to which prefixes, suffixes, and other endings have been added. A base word can stand alone, while a root cannot. For example, in the word *unreasonable*, *reason* is a base word. In the word *construction*, *struct* is a root.

Read each group of words. Circle the two words in each group that have the same base word or root.

1. inspection	perspective	perspiring	**4.** arrangement	prearranged	preparation
2. mistaken	misadventure	adventurous	**5.** immortalize	lamenting	mortician
3. appearance	apprentice	disappeared	**6.** structure	construct	contest

SYNONYMS

Words that have the same meaning are synonyms. Some words that are synonyms, however, have slightly different shades of meaning, even though the general meaning is the same. For example, *change* and *alter* are synonyms, but look at these sentences:

Once I am married, I will <u>change</u> my last name.

Once I am married, I will <u>alter</u> my last name.

The word *change* better fits the intended meaning of the sentence, which is that the person will have a completely new last name. When you alter something, you make it different in a smaller way than when you change it.

Write the word that better fits the meaning of each sentence.

1. I'm taking my parents to a _____ restaurant for their anniversary. (fancy, gaudy)

2. I love your dress! It's so _____! (colorful, flashy)

3. The party and presents were such a nice _____. (shock, surprise)

4. I admire how hard you work. You are a very _____ student. (stubborn, determined)

5. It's a good idea to _____ part of every paycheck every week. (save, hoard)

6. We're going to our _____ in the country for the weekend. (cabin, shack)

7. I decided to bring my umbrella on my _____ to the grocery store. (voyage, trip)

8. The sneaky puppy _____ the cookie out of the toddler's hand. (snatched, took)

GREEK ROOTS

Many English words have Greek roots. Knowing the meanings of Greek roots can help you figure out the meanings of unfamiliar words. Look at these common Greek roots, their meanings, and examples of English words based on them:

bio (life) + *logy* (study of) = *biology*   *auto* (self) + *graph* (write) = *autograph*

Write four words that include these Greek roots: *bio*, *logy*, *auto*, *graph*. Use each root at least once. Then find each word in a dictionary and write a short definition.

1. _____ Dictionary definition: _____
_____

2. _____ Dictionary definition: _____
_____

3. _____ Dictionary definition: _____
_____

4. _____ Dictionary definition: _____
_____

ACADEMIC VOCABULARY

Knowing these high-frequency words will help you in many school subjects.

fact   a piece of information that can be shown to be true or false

opinion   someone's thoughts or beliefs about something

prove   to show the existence, truth, or validity of

viewpoint   a particular attitude or way of thinking about something

reliable   of good quality and able to be trusted

Complete the sentences below using one of the words above.

1. The reviewer had a poor _____ of the new restaurant.

2. My cancelled check will _____ that I paid you.

3. Websites that end in *.edu* are usually _____.

4. When arguing, try to think about things from your opponent's _____.

5. Show me the book where you found that _____ about Neptune.

Lesson 3.6

Identify Genre

The term genre refers to a category or type of art. There are genres of music, film, and literature. Prose, poetry, and drama comprise the main literary genres. Within each genre are a number of subgenres, which are divisions into which each main genre is split.

Prose includes writing that is similar to everyday speech and language. It includes fiction and nonfiction.

- Fiction is imaginary writing, although the characters may seem real or even be real people. Most fiction is written in the form of a novel or a short story, although there are other forms as well. Some kinds of fiction include science fiction, romance, myth, mystery, adventure, and folktale. Historical fiction is a special subgenre that tells stories about real people or events in an imaginative way.

- Nonfiction deals with real people, places, and events. In general, nonfiction texts should be accurate. They may not contain imaginary facts or events. Biographies, autobiographies, memoirs, newspaper and magazine articles, and reports are types of nonfiction. Other types include diary entries, letters, and essays.

Poetry differs from prose by emphasizing the line rather than the sentence. Poets paint pictures of ideas or images, using carefully chosen words and sounds. A poem may or may not rhyme. It may be long or short, creating one image or many images. It may also be sung as a song.

Drama is a story meant to be performed by actors before an audience. When the drama is presented, the actors speak and act as the characters. Drama can be a skit, play, movie, radio play, or television show.

Read the passage about Benjamin Franklin. To what genre or subgenre does it belong?

> Benjamin grumbled as he fished a tiny *h* out of the tray of lead letters. He was sorry he had ever expressed interest in his brother's newspaper. Working at the *New-England Courant* was not as exciting as he had imagined. He set the next line of text and let his mind drift to the next Dogood essay he was planning.

This passage is historical fiction. It is written about Benjamin Franklin—a real person—but it imagines thoughts and actions that may not have happened exactly as they are written.

**Read each passage. Identify its genre or subgenre by writing *poetry*, *fiction*, *drama*, *essay*,
or *myth*. Explain why you selected that genre or subgenre.**

> *(Shanti sets the mug down on the table.)*
>
> Shanti: There is your tea. I hope you choke on it.
>
> Ajay: *(calmly)* I believe I will be able to drink this without injury. *(He takes a sip.)*
> I thank you for the tea.
>
> Shanti: I don't understand how you can be so calm. *(picks up saucer)*
>
> Ajay: I hope you don't plan to throw that. It would be very difficult for you to get
> the shards of pottery out from the cracks in the floor later.

1. _____

> Karima drew her laser pistol and hid it behind her back. She crouched down behind
> the boulder, rearranging her boots and hoping that her whole body was concealed.
> The klandon beast had sharp eyes but practically no sense of smell. She could hear
> it snarling on the other side of the rocks as it looked for her, and she was sure its
> poisonous saliva was dripping from its front fangs. She gripped her pistol and
> debated whether it would be wise to use her communicator to call her ship for help.

2. _____

> Atalanta was a woman warrior who vowed never to marry. So she came up with
> a plan that any man who wanted to marry her had to enter a footrace against her.
> If he won, Atalanta would marry him, but if he lost, he would be put to death.
> Despite these high stakes, many men came to race Atalanta, and all of them died
> because they could not match her speed. One day, a man named Milanion fell in
> love with Atalanta, but he knew that he could never beat her. He asked Aphrodite,
> the goddess of love, for help, and she gave him three golden apples. Milanion
> challenged Atalanta to a race, and she accepted, sorry to see another man put to
> death. During the race, Milanion fell behind. He threw a golden apple out as far
> as he could, and Atalanta stopped to pick up the beautiful fruit. He did this three
> times, and every time Atalanta stopped, Milanion would pull ahead until he finally
> won the race.

3. _____

Read each passage. Then circle the letter of the genre or subgenre to which the passage belongs.

The thing I remember most about grade school was having cold legs. At my school, we had to wear a uniform every day no matter what. Boys were nice and warm in navy pants and white button-down shirts. Girls wore plaid skirts and white blouses. Even though temperatures got down below zero some days, we girls had to wear our plaid skirts to school. Of course we were allowed to wear tights, but my mother learned early on that I could win any battle of wills as long as victory involved me not having to wear itchy, horrible tights.

1. A mystery   **C** memoir

   B poetry   **D** drama

Born from summer's sleepy spell,
Autumn has a tale to tell.
Purple, orange, gold, and red
Patches fall from overhead
Like a gaudy dressing gown
That's torn and tossed down on the ground.
Then brightly colored shreds turn brown,
A chill descends upon the town.
The cold to which all life succumbs—
Autumn's over, winter comes.

2. F autobiography   **H** romance

   G drama   **J** poetry

Many people consider Christy Mathewson the greatest pitcher in the history of baseball. He made his major-league debut for the New York Giants in 1900, at 19 years old. In the 1905 World Series, Mathewson pitched three complete-game shutouts to help the Giants to victory over the Philadelphia Athletics. He is also famous for developing the fadeaway, the reverse curve pitch that is known today as the screwball.

3. A biography   **C** diary entry

   B poetry   **D** drama

Read the passage. Then circle the letter of the answer to each question.

I got into the elevator car and was immediately unsure whether I should go up at all. Its tiny doorway meant that I had to duck to even get inside, and there were four seats positioned close together with no real room to move. Three other people got in after me, including my girlfriend, who had insisted we ride to the top in the first place. The elevator started going up, and after a few minutes, it started moving diagonally. I should have realized that you can't go up the Arch in a straight line. I grasped my girlfriend's hand, and she patted me on the shoulder, but it didn't make me feel better. When we finally got out of the tiny car and took the last few stairs up, we stepped into a narrow room with tiny windows on each side. My girlfriend flitted around, trying to point out Busch Stadium and the Mississippi River. Looking out the window was the last thing I wanted to do as the giant metal structure swayed gently back and forth in the wind.

1. The language of the passage consists mostly of

  A rhythm and rhyme.

  B narration and action.

  C dialogue.

  D persuasive language.

2. The passage is written by

  F a playwright giving action and dialogue directions.

  G a writer about his own life.

  H a writer about a real person's life.

  J a poet about a friend's experiences.

3. The main feeling this passage conveys is

  A joy.

  B wonder.

  C fear.

  D suspicion.

4. The genre of the passage is

  F science fiction.

  G folktale.

  H poetry.

  J memoir.

5. If the genre of the passage were drama instead, what must be included?

  A description

  B persuasive language

  C dialogue

  D rhyme

6. Which line could be added to the end of the passage?

  F "Beam me out of here now!" he cried into his wristphone.

  G To and fro'/To and fro'.

  H I counted the seconds until it was time to leave.

  J Everyone should visit Mississippi.

Workplace Skill: Understand Genre in Training Materials

Most workplace documents deal with real people, places, and events, so they are in the nonfiction subgenre. Workplace writing typically has a professional tone, and the documents are clear, informative, and well-organized. In many jobs, employees must be able to read, understand, and use the information found in many different kinds of materials, such as reference sources, company policies and procedures, and product descriptions. Employers will provided you with the types of documents you need to be successful in your job.

Read the excerpt from a training manual. Then circle the letter of the answer to each question below the box.

Citywide Financial Services Company
Technical Writers' Training Materials

Section: 14.5
Company Library Resources

As a source of useful information for technical writers, the company library should be utilized as often as needed. A variety of library resources are available to technical writers assigned to prepare reports, financial documents, historical analyses, and presentations. Such technical reports may be requested by various internal departments and individuals as they interact with other departments or with clients. These departments can include marketing, financial services, human resources, and investment counseling. The list below indicates the types of resources available in the company library:

Audiovisual Aids

Photographs
Slides
Videos

Online or Computerized Resources

Computer slideshow presentations
Financial e-learning programs
Web-based sources

Written Materials

Journal articles
Newspaper articles
Biographies
Annual reports
Encyclopedias
Product specification documents

---

1. Which type of document would not be useful if you were writing a report on a client's financial status?

  A annual reports

  B biographies

  C journal articles

  D newspaper articles

2. Which type of workplace document would not be in the nonfiction genre?

  F a biography of the company founder

  G a skit in a training video

  H an annual report with graphs

  J instructions for assembling a new product

Write for Work

Review the types of nonfiction documents available for the technical writer to use in his or her daily work. In a notebook, write a list of the types of nonfiction documents and other materials you have used in previous jobs. Write a paragraph explaining how these types of documents helped you to understand and do your job.

Workplace Extension

Responding to a Problem

Adom Nwosu is one of several inventory managers at his company. His supervisor told him that quality problems were occurring in his department, and Adom was asked to give his input on what he felt was the reason for the quality problem. Adom stated his reasons for what he considered to be the problem. During the course of the conversation, the supervisor informed him that the maintenance, engineering, and second shift staff had differing opinions. At this point, Adom became upset and accused everyone else of being "stupid" and "not really understanding the problem."

Circle the letter of the answer to each question.

1. Adom's reaction shows that he

   A is not a good team player.

   B is often late for work.

   C cares about the feelings of others.

   D is concerned about solving problems.

2. Adom's reaction can best be described as

   F cooperative.

   G calm.

   H defensive.

   J proactive.

3. Adom's supervisor will probably think that

   A Adom should get a raise for his honesty.

   B Adom should be promoted to management.

   C Adom is responsible for the department's problems.

   D the maintenance staff is at fault.

4. The supervisor likely asked for Adom's input

   F so that Adom could solve the problem.

   G to try to understand and solve the problem.

   H so Adom could blame others for the problem.

   J because Adom likes to solve problems.

Write the answer to the question.

5. How should Adom have responded to his supervisor's feedback?

_____

_____

Explore Words

Suffixes are word parts that can be added to the end of many words. Adding a suffix changes the meaning of a base word or root. The suffixes -er, -or, and -ist all mean "someone who." For example, the word *teacher* means "someone who teaches," and the word *artist* means "someone who makes art."

Use the suffix -er, -or, or -ist to write a word for each meaning given.

1. someone who visits _____

2. someone who plays piano _____

3. someone who gardens _____

4. someone who acts _____

SPELLING: HOMOPHONES

Words that sound alike but are spelled differently and have different meanings are homophones. For example, the words *weather* and *whether* are homophones.

Circle the word that completes each sentence. Use a dictionary if you're not sure.

1. You can be (fined, find) for jaywalking.
2. His office is just (threw, through) that door.
3. The doctor is not taking any new (patience, patients).
4. Your (presence, presents) at the meeting is requested.
5. After cheering at the football game, my voice was (horse, hoarse).
6. Riding a (stationery, stationary) bike is boring.

WORD FAMILIES

Words that have the same base word or root belong to the same word family. For example, the words *vision*, *visible*, and *visor* are in the same word family. They each have the Latin root *vis*.

Read each clue. Then circle the word that matches the clue.

1. someone who invents	invention	reinventing	inventor
2. not able to be relied upon	reliant	unreliable	relying
3. without a job	unemployed	unemployable	employment
4. able to be carried	portion	portable	transport

An analogy shows a relationship between two pairs of words. To figure out an analogy, decide how the first pair of words relate to each other. Then, select the most appropriate term that makes the second pair of words have the same relationship.

Look at this analogy: *cold* : *hot* as *young* : *old* The symbol (:) stands for "is to." In this example, both pairs of words are antonyms; they have opposite meanings. Here are two other common kinds of analogies:

- Synonyms: *thin* : *slender* as *fat* : *chubby*. Both pairs have almost the same meaning.
- Parts of a whole: *days* : *week* as *minutes* : *hour*. The first word in each pair represents a portion of the second word.

Write the word that best completes each analogy.

1. *Near* : *far* as *large* : _____ (big, small)

2. *Leaf* : *tree* as *petal* : _____ (flower, stem)

3. *Couch* : *sofa* as *chair* : _____ (seat, cushion)

4. *Hired* : *fired* as *healthy*: _____ (sick, happy)

5. *Arm* : *person* as *wing* : _____ (drumstick, airplane)

ACADEMIC VOCABULARY

Knowing these high-frequency words will help you in many school subjects.

genre	a category of art
prose	written or spoken language in ordinary form
emphasize	to give special importance to
drama	a story meant to be performed by actors before an audience
comprise	to make up

Complete the sentences below using one of the words above.

1. Jacobo found the _____ of the novel easy to read.

2. It is a very different experience, reading _____ rather than watching it.

3. Most bookstores organize their books by _____.

4. Maria thought about buying the bathing suit but was afraid it would _____ her waist.

5. Twenty-six different volumes _____ the set of encyclopedias.

Unit 3 Review

Make Generalizations

A generalization is a statement that applies to many people, events, or situations. To make a generalization, you put together a number of facts or examples to reach a logical conclusion. Look for these signal words: *most, many, few, all, usually,* and *generally*.

Recognize Author's Effect and Intention

Authors reveal their intentions by using style techniques to create a particular effect in their writing. This effect may be intensified by an author's choice of words, sentence structure and length, and punctuation.

Compare and Contrast

Comparing shows how two or more things are alike. Contrasting shows how two or more things are different. Writers often compare and contrast in the same passage. Look for these signal words and phrases to show comparisons: *alike, by comparison, similar to, both, likewise,* and *also*. Look for these signal words and phrases to show contrasts: *different, but, while, however, although, unlike,* and *on the other hand*.

Predict Outcomes

When you read, clues in the text can help you figure out what will happen next. You notice details in the text and then think about your own experiences. You can use this information to predict an outcome.

Identify Fact and Opinion

Facts can be proved. You can look them up or check them in some way. Opinions tell what someone believes or thinks. When you read, it is important to separate facts from opinions.

Identify Genre

The term *genre* refers to a category or type of art in music, film, or literature. The main literary genres are prose, poetry, and drama. Prose includes writing that is similar to everyday speech and language. It includes fiction and nonfiction. Novels and short stories are in the fiction subgenre. Newspapers, reference sources, and workplace writing are factual and in the nonfiction subgenre.

Unit 3 Assessment

Read the passages. Then circle the letter of the answer to each question.

One of the greatest rulers in European history was Charlemagne. He was a medieval Frankish king who became famous because he managed to unite many parts of Europe for the first time since the days of the Roman Empire. Charlemagne was noted for his great size and strength, although his own father was known as Pepin the Short. Charlemagne was far from a predictable man. In Charlemagne's time, a common punishment for defeat was death, yet Charlemagne sometimes spared the lives of his defeated foes. At other times he could be extremely harsh, as in the year 782, when he ordered the beheadings of 4,500 Saxons after they rose up against him.

1. What generalization can you make based on this passage?

   A Charlemagne was a strong leader.

   B Charlemagne was an unusually tall man.

   C Most people were smaller than Charlemagne.

   D Charlemagne was the ruler of the Roman Empire.

2. What opinion about Charlemagne is stated in this passage?

   F He was taller than his father.

   G He united many parts of Europe.

   H He was one of the greatest rulers in European history.

   J He had 4,500 Saxons beheaded in 782.

North Dakota and South Dakota are states that share a common history. Both were originally part of the Dakota Territory, a vast land area officially established in 1861. Both were admitted to the United States of America as individual states on November 2, 1889. The Missouri River runs through the capital cities of both states—Bismarck, North Dakota, and Pierre, South Dakota. Although the two states do have similarities, they are different in many ways. North Dakota can claim an international border with Canada, while South Dakota has no international border. Oil and coal are the key natural resources of North Dakota, whereas gold has been a great claim to fame for South Dakota. Many thousands of tourists visit the Mount Rushmore National Memorial in South Dakota each year. Others visit Rugby, North Dakota, which marks the geographical center of the continent of North America.

3. What is one way North Dakota and South Dakota are alike?

   A Both share a border with another country.

   B Both have capitals built along the Missouri River.

   C Gold is an important resource for both states.

   D Both have sites that mark the center of North America.

4. The second sentence is an example of

   F a comparison.

   G an opinion.

   H a cause.

   J an effect.

True icebergs, as opposed to frozen chunks of sea ice, are composed of fresh water. The ice in the Antarctic icebergs, for instance, was created by the buildup of snow and its compression into ice on the Antarctic continent over the course of many years. This ice flows slowly toward the continent's edge. At the coast, it forms glaciers or ice shelves that can be more than 200 meters thick. Huge chunks of this compressed ice are continually breaking off the coast of Antarctica, forming massive icebergs. Because so much fresh water is contained within these chunks, people have been trying to find ways to extract it for centuries. In 1773 Captain James Cook wrote in his log about harvesting ice from an iceberg. It wasn't hard for him to collect enough ice for his crew to melt and use as drinking water. Collecting enough to help the millions of people in dry areas of the world is quite another challenge. Scientists and creative thinkers have made many proposals, including suggestions about how to tow icebergs to shore. So far, no one has successfully accomplished this goal.

5. What do you predict will happen to iceberg research?

  A People will stop thinking about the fresh water contained in icebergs.

  B People will keep trying to find ways to get fresh water from icebergs.

  C People will hire sea captains to harvest ice from icebergs.

  D People will decide that icebergs have no practical value.

6. What generalization can you make based on this passage?

  F All people need fresh water.

  G Captain James Cook used an iceberg as a source of fresh water.

  H One idea scientists have considered is to tow icebergs to shore.

  J A true iceberg is not a frozen chunk of sea ice.

Few people are aware of the amazing accomplishment of Sybil Ludington, a courageous 16-year-old girl who made a daring ride during the Revolutionary War. Two years after Paul Revere and others famously rode through Massachusetts to warn farmers about British troops, the war was still raging. On April 26, 1777, the commander of a military regiment in New York received word that British troops were attacking the nearby town of Danbury, Connecticut. All the local farmers would be needed for the coming fight. Who could spread the word? The commander's eldest daughter volunteered for the task. Sybil Ludington rode her horse over 40 miles through the dark night, alerting the inhabitants to the coming danger. Sybil returned home safely, and the militia stopped the British advance.

7. What is the subgenre of this passage?

  A autobiography

  B biography

  C folktale

  D mystery

8. The author's intention in writing this passage is

  F to prove that Sybil Ludington was more important than Paul Revere.

  G to make fun of Sybil Ludington.

  H to describe a little-known historical figure.

  J to explain how the Revolutionary War was won.

The green basilisk is one type of lizard found in Central America. Like other lizards, it is a reptile and has a scaly body. This reptile lives near water, often spending time in nearby trees. However, it is on the water that the basilisk shows a distinct difference from most other lizards. At the end of its long, thin legs, the toes of a basilisk have special flaps, or fringes, that can spread out like a web. When a basilisk is fleeing from an enemy, it can drop out of a tree and literally run across the surface of the water in order to make a quick getaway.

9. In this passage, how is the basilisk contrasted to other types of lizards?

   A   It can run along the surface of the water.

   B   It is a reptile.

   C   It has a scaly body.

   D   It is found in Central America.

10. The genre or subgenre of this passage can best be described as

    F   drama.

    G   fiction.

    H   nonfiction.

    J   poetry.

(1) I think it is really sad that many people choose to stay in impersonal hotels and motels instead of old-fashioned country inns. (2) In many countries, it has long been a custom for people to offer their own homes as places for travelers to stay. (3) Even today, many individuals open bed-and-breakfast establishments, offering a good meal, a comfortable bed, and pleasant conversation. (4) Unfortunately, the building of railroads led to the building of new hotels along their tracks. (5) The building of highways led to the motel, or motor hotel. (6) Motels are usually located right next to noisy, busy highways. (7) There is little hint of true hospitality in such places, but it must be said that motels do offer inexpensive lodging.

11. Which sentence uses descriptive details to create a comforting effect?

    A   sentence 3

    B   sentence 4

    C   sentence 5

    D   sentence 6

12. Which sentence contains both a fact *and* an opinion?

    F   sentence 2

    G   sentence 5

    H   sentence 6

    J   sentence 7

Read the bulletin board notice. Then circle the letter of the answer to each question.

Severe Weather Procedures—
PLEASE READ

At Briarly, Lopez, and Li, we strive to serve our clients fully and completely. We plan staffing to ensure that services and operations are smoothly maintained throughout the workday. In the event that severe weather should compromise the usual schedule, please follow the process outlined below for the safety and convenience of both staff and clients.

StormMessage System

To learn about late opening hours, early closing hours, or a shutdown of our offices, you have two options:

1. Call 555-555-7200 to hear a recorded weather-alert message, which will be available by 6:30 A.M. Central Standard Time.

2. Visit our website at www.briarlylopezli.com and click on the flashing weather-alert message button for details. A direct link to the StormResponse System is also provided.

StormResponse System

- If severe weather makes it unsafe for you to travel to the office, call or send an e-mail to inform the following parties: your direct manager, the receptionist, your direct team members, and human resources. This message must be sent by 7 A.M. Central Standard Time.

- If a client appointment will be impacted by this absence, it is imperative that relevant information be provided in the message. The client will be notified so as to avoid any misunderstanding or inconvenience.

13. What generalization can you make about the company based on this notice?

   A   The company prepares carefully for emergencies.

   B   The company cares only about clients, not employees.

   C   The company is not open during severe weather.

   D   The company requires employees to come to work in severe weather.

14. How are the two options of the StormMessage System alike?

   F   Both require accessing the company website.

   G   Both require making a phone call.

   H   Both provide a weather-alert message.

   J   Both contain a direct link to the StormResponse System.

15. What is the most likely outcome of not following the process outlined in the notice?

   A   You may be caught in a traffic jam.

   B   You may miss an appointment with a client.

   C   You may sleep late.

   D   Your colleagues may work overtime.

16. What is NOT the intention of the writer of this notice?

   F   to urge employees to make decisions based on personal safety

   G   to make sure all colleagues are aware of each others' plans

   H   to stress the importance of maintaining client services

   J   to provide employees with an excuse to skip work

Read the job postings. Then circle the letter of the answer to each question.

Job Posting 1: Associate Production Editor

Duties and Responsibilities Take a coordinating role in the creation of high-quality print and digital products. Follow lead of Senior Production Editor in maintaining high-quality standards throughout publishing process. Track all aspects of production process, including manuscript submission and art/photo lists. Proofread assigned manuscripts for accuracy of content and for implementation of all project guidelines. Work closely with Senior Production Editor and managers of other departments. Train and monitor work of Production Editorial Assistant.

Required Experience Moderate experience in all facets of publications production, including good familiarity with current technology. Strong organizational skills, with an emphasis on prioritizing. Excellent communication skills. Ability to work both independently and as part of a team.

Minimum Qualifications Two or more years of work experience in the field of publications or four-year college degree in design, communications, or related field.

Job Posting 2: Production Editorial Assistant

Duties and Responsibilities Support Associate Production Editor in the creation of high-quality print and digital products. Create word processing files (documents, charts) as assigned. Proofread for accuracy of all content, including headers, file names, etc. Prepare tracking charts for all aspects of page production process, including manuscript submission and art/photo lists. Perform administrative tasks (photocopying, preparing electronic transmittals, answering phones) as needed.

Required Experience Interest in the field of publications. Familiarity with current office technology. Strong organizational skills and communication skills. Ability to work as part of a team.

Minimum Qualifications Two-year college degree in design, communications, or related field or equivalent experience. Four-year college degree a plus.

---

17. What is a likely outcome for the person who is hired for the job of Associate Production Editor?

   A   He or she will train the person hired for the Production Editorial Assistant job.

   B   He or she will learn how to prioritize.

   C   He or she will track art/photo lists.

   D   He or she will perform administrative tasks.

18. What generalization can you make based on these two job postings?

   F   Production editors never work with other departments.

   G   Production editors need excellent communication skills.

   H   Production editors must study design in college.

   J   Production editors work mainly on print products.

Circle the letter of the answer to each question.

19. Which two words are NOT homophones?

    A stares, stairs

    B brine, bring

    C vain, vein

    D flour, flower

20. Which word is a synonym for *trounced*?

    F decided

    G traded

    H defeated

    J requested

21. Which word contains the schwa sound?

    A awake

    B remake

    C biplane

    D empty

22. Which word fits into both sentences?

    Our daily _____ is twice as big now that we are using new fishing equipment.

    Ocean sailors are always relieved to _____ the first glimpse of land.

    F gather

    G catch

    H patch

    J spy

23. Which word means "to make powerful"?

    A implore

    B endanger

    C embolden

    D empower

24. Which word means "the act of adopting"?

    F adopts

    G adopted

    H adoption

    J adopt

25. Which phrase defines the underlined word in the sentence? Use context clues to help you figure it out.

    I was not surprised that Hanh became a <u>geriatric</u> counselor since she has always enjoyed spending time with her grandparents.

    A pertaining to grief

    B pertaining to the elderly

    C the act of giving

    D the act of sharing

26. Which word best completes the following analogy?

    Early : late as *rough* : _____

    F smooth

    G sturdy

    H rowdy

    J tough

27. Which word has a prefix, a suffix, and a Latin root?

    A extreme

    B cleaner

    C traveling

    D importer

28. Which plural word is spelled correctly?

    F photo's

    G photos

    H photoes

    J photoss

29. Which word is an antonym for *confident*?

    A uncertain

    B sure

    C secretive

    D friendly

30. Which word means "to bring together as one"?

    F create

    G believe

    H undo

    J unify

Posttest

Read each passage. Then circle the letter of the answer to each question.

> There were more than 1,500 people onboard, and every one of them was intending to have a good time. It happened on the third night at sea during the captain's gala when the women wore elegant gowns and glamorous jewels. They couldn't have looked more beautiful. At first the waiters began to have trouble balancing their trays full of dishes. Then the waves started to wash over the main deck, and soon after that, the vessel began to tilt dangerously. It was then that the captain radioed for help. A passenger later recalled, "All I remember is water rising and almost knocking me over. When the emergency warning sounded, I left my cabin and started toward the lifeboat station. Then I saw those children at the end of the hall, and I knew I couldn't leave them. I waded into the hall—it wasn't easy because the ship was rocking—but somehow I got to them."

1. Which character trait best describes the passenger who is quoted?

   A selfless

   B ignorant

   C selfish

   D intelligent

2. When did the captain radio for help?

   F when the ship began to tilt

   G before the waves washed over the main deck

   H right after waiters had trouble balancing their trays

   J when the emergency warning sounded

3. Which style technique is NOT used in the passage?

   A description

   B short sentences

   C dialogue

   D action

4. You can conclude that the events in the passage took place

   F in a restaurant.

   G on a cruise ship.

   H on a remote island.

   J on an airplane.

5. What effect is created by the author's use of language?

   A danger

   B calm

   C anger

   D wonder

6. What caused the ship to start rocking?

   F It hit an iceberg.

   G A tidal wave washed over it.

   H It ran into a powerful storm.

   J not stated

7. What do you predict the man will do next?

   A He will stay where he is and wait for help.

   B He will lead the children to the lifeboat station.

   C The water will drain out of the boat.

   D The man will leave without the children.

8. Which statement expresses an opinion?

   F There were more than 1,500 people onboard.

   G The waves started to wash over the main deck.

   H The captain radioed for help.

   J The women couldn't have looked more beautiful.

You've probably heard the expression *sly as a fox*. How did the fox get its reputation for being a clever animal? The reputation may have begun with fox hunters. A hunter tries to catch a fox by chasing it on a horse. The hunter sends a pack of hound dogs ahead to find the fox, and the dogs pick up the fox's scent and chase it. Rather than slipping into the nearest thicket, the fox may keep running to keep the chase alive. If one of a pair of foxes is being chased, its mate may dash out of a hiding place and lead the pursuers in another direction. By crossing streams, running along the tops of fences, and darting through the woods, a pair of foxes can keep a pack of hounds totally confused—at least for a while.

9. Which sentence states the main idea of the passage?

   A   Foxes cannot run as fast as hounds.

   B   Some people think that fox hunting is a cruel sport.

   C   Dogs pick up a fox's scent and chase it down.

   D   Foxes' reputation for being sly may come from their actual behavior.

10. From this passage you can conclude that foxes survive a hunt by

   F   being smarter than the hounds.

   G   being stronger than the hounds.

   H   running faster than the hounds.

   J   hiding in the forest.

11. Which is the best summary of this passage?

   A   Foxes are sly, but hounds are faster runners. A fox is no match for a hound's speed and sense of smell.

   B   When they are being hunted, foxes use clever tactics to avoid capture. They can confuse hounds enough to get away at least some of the time.

   C   Foxes and hounds are natural enemies, which is why hunters use hounds to find foxes.

   D   Hunters use hounds to chase foxes because they aren't smart enough to find them on their own.

12. Which concept is implied but NOT stated in the passage?

   F   Foxes don't deserve their reputation for being sly.

   G   Foxes are smarter and more agile than hounds.

   H   Hounds never catch the foxes they chase.

   J   Hounds are successful at catching foxes much of the time.

Are you interested in our city's history? If the answer is "yes," you should join the protest against the construction of high-rise apartment buildings in the downtown area! This unnecessary housing project would replace a row of historic shops that date from the early 1900s and that are the backbone of the downtown shopping area. We mustn't let this happen! The housing plan also makes no provision for parking or pedestrian traffic. It seems to have been created with only one thing in mind—to line the pockets of wealthy developers who have no vested interest in our community. All who consider themselves good citizens of Oak Creek should actively work to block the construction of these apartments.

13. Which sentence could be added to the paragraph to support the main idea?

- **A** People generally spend too much in shops, anyway.
- **B** The shops add very little to the cultural life of the city.
- **C** The buildings that house the shops are crumbling.
- **D** The shop owners have been a part of our city for decades.

14. Which statement expresses an opinion?

- **F** There is no provision for parking.
- **G** This is an unnecessary housing project.
- **H** It will replace a row of shops.
- **J** High-rise apartment buildings will be built.

15. Readers are most likely to find this selection

- **A** on the editorial page of a newspaper.
- **B** in a personal journal.
- **C** in a book of poetry.
- **D** in a history textbook.

16. Based on the passage, what do you predict the writer might do?

- **F** move to a new community
- **G** campaign for a candidate who is in favor of preserving the historic downtown area
- **H** follow the progress of the apartment project by reading the weekly newspaper
- **J** purchase an apartment when the project is complete

17. What style technique does the author use in this passage?

- **A** punctuation
- **B** short sentences
- **C** dialogue
- **D** action

18. Which concept is stated in the passage?

- **F** The plan makes no provision for parking.
- **G** Other towns have stopped housing projects.
- **H** Oak Creek was established in the early 1900s.
- **J** Good citizens enjoy downtown shopping.

A cat's whiskers are important because they are extremely sensitive sense organs. Whiskers help a cat judge the width of tight spaces in order to know whether it is possible to squeeze through. Whiskers also work like weather vanes—they can tell a cat which way the wind is blowing. More importantly, the stimulation of a cat's whiskers triggers a blinking reflex. For example, if a jutting twig or other hazard touches the whiskers, the cat blinks its eyes. The blinking protects the eyes from damage. If you have a cat, you can see this reflex by lightly brushing the cat's whiskers.

19. The writer compares a cat's whiskers to a

   A blinking eye.

   B weather vane.

   C tight space.

   D jutting twig.

20. What is the main idea of this paragraph?

   F Cats have quick reflexes.

   G Cats can fit in small places if they rely on their whiskers.

   H Cats are not the only animals who have whiskers.

   J Cats' whiskers are highly sensitive to the sense of touch.

21. What could be added to the passage to act as supporting evidence for the main idea?

   A A cat's tongue has special spines on it to assist in grooming.

   B A cat's ears can turn more quickly than a dog's ears can.

   C Many cats groom one another as a sign of affection.

   D A cat will be temporarily disabled if its whiskers are cut off.

22. As used in this passage, the word *sensitive* means

   F "affected by slight changes."

   G "easily offended or upset."

   H "kept secret for reasons of security."

   J "particularly aware of others' feelings."

The blue-footed booby is a bird with blue feet. The males show off their bright blue feet to attract a mate, performing a high-stepping strut for females. The name booby comes from the Spanish word *bobo*, which means "stupid." The birds were named boobies by Europeans who had traveled to the parts of Central and South America where the boobies live. The blue-footed booby looks funnier than most European birds.

23. What is the author's purpose for writing this passage?

   A to persuade readers that the blue-footed booby is smarter than people realize

   B to explain the life cycle of the blue-footed booby

   C to describe an interesting bird

   D to entertain with a funny story about birds

24. Which statement is an opinion?

   F The blue-footed booby is a bird with blue feet.

   G The males show off their bright blue feet to attract a mate.

   H The name booby comes from the Spanish word *bobo*.

   J The blue-footed booby looks funnier than most European birds.

Posttest continued

Read the glossary excerpt. Then circle the letter of the answer to each question.

> ## Glossary
> **samba**   an Afro-Brazilian dance
>
> **sarangi**   a stringed instrument from north India
>
> **ska**   a type of Jamaican urban music
>
> **swing**   big-band jazz music
>
> **tag**   a jazz term for a final section of music
>
> **timbales**   drums of Cuban origin, usually played in pairs
>
> **timbrel**   an ancient percussion instrument similar to a tambourine

25. Suppose the writer wants to add the word *tempo* to the glossary. Which word would follow it?

   A swing

   B tag

   C timbales

   D timbrel

26. What is most likely the genre of the book that contains this glossary?

   F fiction

   G drama

   H poetry

   J nonfiction

Read the passage. Then circle the letter of the answer to each question.

> If you're like the average American adult, you probably eat about 22 teaspoons of sugar every day. That much sugar is more than twice the recommended amount. Even when you try to avoid sugar, you're probably eating a lot more than you think you are. Soft drinks, candy, ice cream, and cupcakes are obvious sources of sugar. But if you really want to avoid sugar, you'll have to say "no" to ketchup, frozen dinners, salad dressing, hot dogs, and packaged breads. Sugar is added to those foods and many others when they are processed.

27. What generalization can you make from this passage?

   A People should be aware of the sugar in their diet.

   B Most Americans eat too many hot dogs.

   C Most dietary sugar comes from ketchup.

   D Any amount of sugar is unhealthy.

28. The writing style of this passage creates an effect of

   F suspense.

   G humor.

   H authority.

   J uncertainty.

Posttest continued

Read the product label. Then circle the letter of the answer to each question.

Drug Facts

USES Temporarily relieves the following symptoms due to hay fever or other upper respiratory allergies:
• sneezing • runny nose • itchy throat • itchy, watery eyes

WARNING Ask a doctor before using if
• you have glaucoma • you have a breathing problem such as asthma
• you are taking tranquilizers or sedatives

WHEN USING THIS PRODUCT
• you may get drowsy • avoid alcoholic drinks
• be careful when driving or when operating machinery
• excitability may occur, especially in children

DIRECTIONS Do not take more than 4 doses in 24 hours, as follows:

Adults and children 12 years and over	2 tablets every 4–6 hours
Children 6 to 12 years	1 tablet every 4–6 hours
Children under 6 years	Ask a doctor before using.

Other information • Store at 68–77°F • Protect from excessive moisture

29. What is the maximum number of tablets an adult may take in 24 hours?

A 2

B 4

C 8

D 12

30. You would find this type of label on

F a piece of furniture.

G a food item.

H an over-the-counter drug.

J an appliance.

31. What may happen to children who use this product?

A They may need more than four doses in 24 hours.

B They may become excitable.

C They may become sedated.

D They may develop a runny nose.

32. Taking this product may cause

F drowsiness.

G breathing problems.

H an itchy throat.

J glaucoma.

One type of domestic goat is the fainting goat. These goats have a condition called myotonia, which can cause them to stiffen and fall over when startled. Goats that have fainted stay in this condition for up to 15 seconds. Then the animal gets up and walks off stiffly. When the stiffness goes away, it's as if nothing happened at all.

33. What is the author's purpose for writing this passage?

A to describe where goats live

B to persuade readers to raise goats

C to entertain readers with an exciting story

D to inform readers about the fainting goats

34. When a goat faints, it is the result of

F nothing at all.

G being startled.

H stiffness.

J falling over.

Posttest continued

Read the workplace document from a phone sales training manual. Then circle the letter of the answer to each question.

Remember that your call is probably interrupting the prospect's busy day. You have only 10 to 15 seconds to get a prospect's attention during a cold call. Therefore, it makes sense to make the most of those precious few seconds. These tips and techniques can help make every call successful.

1. Begin with a simple greeting, such as "Good morning, Mr. Costanza." Avoid familiarity if you don't already have a relationship with the prospect. Do **not** ask, "How are you today?"

2. Customize your greeting according to the person you are calling and where he or she is located. For example, suppose you are calling a law firm. Continue by saying, "This is Michelle Nugyen calling from Affordable Office Solutions *here in Fort Lee*. We *specialize in working with law firms*. I'd like to ask a few questions to see if our service might be of interest to you."

3. Do not say anything that will make your prospect or client feel wrong or stupid. For example, do **not** ask, "Would you like to save money on office supplies?" The question is designed to make the customer say "yes" or else sound wrong or stupid, but this kind of manipulation doesn't work. Instead, ask, "Do you have a moment to talk?" That question asks for permission to continue. Clients will stay on the phone if they feel that they are in control.

35. The first thing a seller should do when making a cold call is

   A greet the person who answers simply.

   B ask the person who answers if he or she is the owner.

   C ask, "How are you today?"

   D ask a question that must be answered "yes."

36. As used in the document, *tips* means

   F "falls over."

   G "money left for a waiter."

   H "the pointed ends of something."

   J "helpful pieces of advice."

37. Cold callers should always avoid

   A calling during the dinner hours.

   B interrupting someone's work day.

   C asking for permission to continue.

   D making someone feel wrong or stupid.

38. Based on the document, which statement is a valid generalization?

   F The most important job is making customers feel smart.

   G Most successful sellers are very aggressive.

   H Most successful sellers prepare before each cold call.

   J All potential customers have to be manipulated into buying.

39. What is the main idea of the last tip?

   A Be sure to ask if your client wants to save money.

   B Do not make your client feel wrong or stupid.

   C Always ask for permission to continue speaking.

   D Customize your greeting.

40. What conclusion can you draw about cold calls?

   F It is easy to get a prospect to stay on the line.

   G You need to be aggressive to make a sale.

   H Don't worry if you make someone feel stupid.

   J It is not always easy to make a sale during a cold call.

Posttest continued

Read the workplace document from a job safety manual. Then circle the letter of the answer to each question.

> Back injuries are the number one workplace injury. One in five on-the-job injuries involves the back. Back injuries can lead to permanent disability, loss of work, and expensive medical bills. To avoid injury to the back while working in the warehouse, follow the rules for safe lifting.
>
> 1. Stretch gently to loosen muscles before lifting.
> 2. Size up the load and test it to see whether you can safely lift it. Get a solid grip, make sure your footing is secure, and maintain your balance.
> 3. Get close to the load and keep the weight close to your body while lifting.
> 4. Lift with your legs, not your back. Bend your knees, keep your back straight, and lift slowly and smoothly.
> 5. Never twist at the waist or hips while lifting.
> 6. Watch for obstacles to make sure you have a clear path.
> 7. Release the load the same way you picked it up, with knees bent and back straight.
> 8. Never attempt to move extremely heavy or awkward objects alone. Ask for help instead.

41. What should you NOT do when lifting?

  A Ask for help.

  B Bend your knees.

  C Twist at the waist or hips.

  D Keep your back straight.

42. What was the author's purpose for writing this document?

  F to instruct workers how to lift properly

  G to persuade workers not to file disability claims

  H to describe the signs of a back injury

  J to tell a story about someone who hurt her back

43. How many work-related injuries involve the back?

  A one in ten

  B half

  C one in five

  D eight in ten

44. As used in the document, the word *clear* means

  F "easy to understand."

  G "transparent."

  H "free of unwanted objects."

  J "not cloudy."

45. What should you do first if you need to lift something heavy?

  A Bend your knees.

  B Size up the load.

  C Stretch your muscles.

  D Get close to the load.

46. What is the best paraphrase of the last point of the document?

  F You should get help for anything you plan to lift.

  G Ask for help if you need to move something that is very heavy or has an awkward shape.

  H It's fine to lift extremely heavy items, but if something has an odd shape, get help.

  J You can do heavy lifting even if it's not safe.

Posttest continued

Circle the letter of the word that is spelled correctly.

47. My dentist discovered three _____ during my annual check-up.

    A cavityies

    B cavitees

    C cavities

    D caviteies

48. That package is much _____ than this one.

    F heavier

    G heavyier

    H heaver

    J heavyer

49. We placed a holiday _____ on our front door.

    A reathe

    B wreath

    C wreeth

    D wreate

50. Katrina _____ vote because she didn't register in time.

    F couldn't

    G culn't

    H couldnt

    J coudn't

51. These boots keep me from _____ on ice.

    A slideing

    B sliding

    C sliddeing

    D slidding

52. She sews with very small _____.

    F stitchs

    G stitchies

    H stitchess

    J stitches

Circle the letter of the answer to each question.

53. Which two words are homophones?

    A moan, mourn

    B wade, weighed

    C duck, drake

    D paper, pauper

54. Which phrase means "the SUV that belongs to my boss"?

    F my bosses SUV

    G my boss's SUV

    H my boss SUV

    J my boss' SUV

55. Which word fits in both sentences?

    Coconuts come from _____ trees.

    I can hold the kitten in the _____ of my hand.

    A maple

    B palm

    C pine

    D apple

56. Which word has an open first syllable?

    F fragrance

    G fixture

    H fancy

    J festive

57. Which word does NOT have a long *e* vowel sound?

    A field

    B eight

    C speed

    D speak

58. Which word begins with a consonant blend?

    F salad

    G gather

    H really

    J grateful

59. Which word has an *r*-controlled vowel sound?

  A restful

  B sunrise

  C daybreak

  D morning

60. Which two words have the same root?

  F transport, portable

  G piece, portion

  H table, chair

  J probable, possible

61. Which is a synonym of the word *furious*?

  A frightened

  B happy

  C angry

  D forgiving

62. Which word does NOT have a silent consonant?

  F knuckle

  G limb

  H tumble

  J science

63. Which two words are antonyms?

  A bravery, courage

  B poor, destitute

  C return, release

  D adverse, beneficial

64. Which word means "partly private"?

  F preprivate

  G disprivate

  H triprivate

  J semiprivate

65. What is the meaning of the prefix *dis-*?

  A not

  B below

  C before

  D half

66. Which word begins with the same sound as *sandwich*?

  F citizen

  G coastal

  H cabbage

  J shutter

67. Which word means "tending to react"?

  A reactish

  B reactive

  C reactly

  D reactment

68. Which word is the base word in *misbehavior*?

  F havior

  G behavior

  H misbehave

  J behave

69. Which word begins with the same sound as *jealous*?

  A gangster

  B guitar

  C gentleman

  D goodness

Circle the letter of the word that completes each analogy.

70. *Checkers* : *game* as *tangerine* : _____.

  F sour

  G seeds

  H fruit

  J round

71. *Milk* : *refrigerator* as _____ : *closet*.

  A book

  B shirt

  C ice cream

  D car

POSTTEST EVALUATION CHART AND ANSWER KEY

This posttest was designed to check your mastery of the reading skills studied. Use the key on page 200 to check your answers. Then circle the question numbers that you answered incorrectly and review the practice pages covering those skills. Carefully rework those practice pages to be sure you understand those skills.

Tested Skills	Question Numbers	Practice Pages
Recognize and Recall Details	29, 37, 41, 43	14–17
Understand Stated Concepts	12, 18	22–25
Draw Conclusions	4, 10, 40	30–33
Summarize and Paraphrase	11, 46	38–41
Identify Cause and Effect	6, 31, 32, 34	46–49
Identify Style Techniques	3, 17	54–57
Find the Main Idea	9, 20, 39	62–65
Identify Sequence	2, 35, 45	78–81
Understand Consumer Materials	29–32	86–89
Use Reference Sources/Indexes	25, 26	94–97
Recognize Character Traits	1	102–105
Use Supporting Evidence	13, 21	110–113
Identify Author's Purpose	23, 33, 42	118–121
Make Generalizations	27, 38	134–137
Identify Author's Effect and Intention	5, 28	142–145
Compare and Contrast	19	150–153
Predict Outcomes	7, 16	158–161
Identify Fact and Opinion	8, 14, 24	166–169
Identify Genre	15, 26	174–177
Synonyms/Antonyms	61, 63	20, 28, 84, 124, 172
Context Clues	22, 36, 44, 55	29, 45, 69, 93, 109, 141, 165
Spelling	47–54	28, 37, 52, 60, 68, 85, 92, 100, 116, 124, 149, 180
Phonics/Word Analysis	56–60, 62, 64–71	20, 21, 28, 36, 44, 52, 53, 60, 61, 68, 84, 92, 101, 108, 117, 124, 125, 140, 148, 156, 157, 164, 172, 173, 180, 181

KEY			
1.	A	39.	B
2.	F	40.	J
3.	B	41.	C
4.	G	42.	F
5.	A	43.	C
6.	J	44.	H
7.	B	45.	C
8.	J	46.	G
9.	D	47.	C
10.	F	48.	F
11.	B	49.	B
12.	G	50.	F
13.	D	51.	B
14.	G	52.	J
15.	A	53.	B
16.	G	54.	G
17.	A	55.	B
18.	F	56.	F
19.	B	57.	B
20.	J	58.	J
21.	D	59.	D
22.	F	60.	F
23.	C	61.	C
24.	J	62.	H
25.	C	63.	D
26.	J	64.	J
27.	A	65.	A
28.	H	66.	F
29.	C	67.	B
30.	H	68.	J
31.	B	69.	C
32.	F	70.	H
33.	D	71.	B
34.	G		
35.	A		
36.	J		
37.	D		
38.	H		